# INDONESIA

# INDONESIA
## Society and Politics

Ganganath Jha

SHIPRA

ISBN: 81-7541-151-1

First Published in India in 2003

Indonesia: Society and Politics



*Published by:*
SHIPRA PUBLICATIONS
115-A, Shakarpur, Vikas Marg
Delhi-110092, INDIA
Phone: 22458662, 22500954
Fax: 91-11-22458662
E-mail: siprapub@satyam.net.in
www.shiprapublications.com

*Laser typesetting by:*
Kumar DTP Systems
Delhi-110091

*Printed at:*
Choudhary Offset Process
Delhi-110051

# Preface

This is an attempt to analyse the intricacies of some aspects of Indonesian society and politics which have proved unique and interesting. A Muslim Community outside finds it astounding that Islam is not declared state religion in Indonesia despite the presence of overwhelming number of Muslims. Although there is a large number of extremist elements and political organisations in the country who advocate orthodox Islamic laws for governance, but moderate elements are too overwhelming to obey it. Java and Bali, where 65 percent of the population resides, have liberal Muslims and they are supportive of secular and humanistic approach. Muslims in that area rarely offer *Namaz* five times a day. They profess Islamic ideals, but abstain from its orthodoxy in their daily life. Their favourite epics are *Ramayana* and *Mahabharata* and their national symbols are derived from those epics. Their *Mahabarata* and *Ramayana* slightly differ from Indian counterparts, and is more popularised through shadow plays (*Wayang*) throughout the country for centuries. It is an anecdote that some of the heroes of the *Mahabharata* were reborn in Indonesia and it was due to their efforts that Islam became acceptable. There are stories of *Arjuna*, *Karna*, *Ghatotkach* and *Hanuman* linked with Islamic characters, which depict a wonderful communion of Islam and Hinduism. Although majority of the people in Bali are Hindus, Indonesians project them as the apostle of their culture and civilisation to the outside world. Some of their national symbols have similarities with India and some words are derived from *Sanskrit*. Those who have faith in Indian mythology and mysticism would be overwhelmed to find similarities in the Indonesian rituals and customs. I, as an observer of Indonesian politics, have a firm belief, that Indonesia would always remain secular and beyond the reach of fundamentalists. The fanatics would have to accept this ground reality sooner or later.

It is in this context that the fanatics have raised the bogey of Javanese domination over other islands. The parallel may be drawn with the situation in India before P.V. Narsimha Rao became the Prime Minister. It was generally understood that only a leader of the North can become the Prime Minister of India. Whoever gets majority in the Hindi heartland would form the government in the Centre. As this region was most populous and politically organised, it dominated over the political horizon for decades but the situation changed in the 1990s. Similarly Javanese hold over Indonesian politics may be strong, but in democracy and coalition politics, various combinations and permutations keep on changing. Indonesia ushered into a democratic era after the downfall of President Suharto (1998). His Successor, B.J. Habibie was not from Java. Various political parties are active in Java now and the votes are bound to be divided. Javanese dominance in political matters can continue only if they are united to support one party, but this is not possible in a democratic system. The evolving democratic institutions would certainly take care of the claims of the opposition that needs to be addressed.

Indonesia is facing unrest in the recent past because of the transition from authoritarian to democratic governance. The Executive, which had usurped powers of the Legislature and Judiciary to a great extent, has been checked under the present system. The Parliament and Supreme court are becoming strong as rule making and rule adjudication bodies. All resolutions are discussed in the parliament and political parties are vibrant with their activities. Although the President is given five years tenure to govern, President Abdurrahaman Wahid was removed on corruption charges much before the expiry of his term. Wahid's selection and removal were the result of high-level political manoeuvring and people's representatives have displayed maturity by selecting a national leader in his place, Megawati Sukarnoputri, to lead the nation. The performance of the government is discussed in the legislature and accountability is fixed for omissions and commissions.

The major problems with which Indonesia is confronted today are the issues of economic development and national integration. President Suharto, known as the father of development, and promoting Berkeley Mafia is defiled, and the growth rates have fallen. The greatest impact of the Asian crisis (1997-98) had been felt on Indonesia, which finally removed President Suharto from power. The struggle for power subsequently amongst the armed forces, political parties and religious groups led to an agenda which threatened the concept of "Unity in diversity". President Habibie, in the meanwhile announced referendum for East Timor without taking Parliament into confidence, and the outcome of referendum was negative for the nation. East Timor became independent and it opened floodgates for similar demands in Aceh, Ambon and Irian Jaya with gusto. The separatists became more enthused and the government proved inadequate in dealing with the complex situation. The worsening economic scenario combined with social and political upheaval have adversely affected the existing order of Indonesia at national and regional levels.

Proper understanding of Indonesian society and politics needs lot of analysis and introspection. The country with 17508 island has a variety of cultures and traditions and is considered anthropologist's paradise. Mysticism plays a great role in social life and there are some visible and invisible factors which have shaped the destiny of the nation. The unity of the nation is threatened and there are some who believe that this country is based on solid unifying factors, like common language, common geographical problems and common literature. On the other hand, there are those who believe that it is too vast and heterogeneous to remain united. They point out that the tendency for fragmentation is natural because of geo-political reasons. Lee Khoon Choy (1999) has argued about the fragility of Indonesia in the backdrop of the history of different islands and ethnic groups. Though the study is interesting, its conclusions are provocative. If multi-ethnic character of Indonesia can be the cause for disintegration, the future of India and China are indeed doomed. They are multi-lingual, multi-culture and multi-religious groups.

They too face separatist movements, but solutions exist for "live and let live". People's welfare is the prime task of the government and the democratic system in letter and spirit would resolve the question of unity in due course.

India and Indonesia have striking similarities of culture, attitudes and life style and they may be projected natural partners. They have common problems of nation building and modernisation and many ideas to share. As an Indian, I am surcharged to find that they still preserve the essence of Hindu culture and civilisation. Even with my limited understanding of Indonesia, I am an admirer of their culture and civilisation and have tried to analyse some salient features and structure of Indonesian society and political ethos. In this endeavour, I am grateful to Prof. Devendra Kaushik, who encouraged me to write on Indonesia and provided useful suggestions. I am also indebted to some Indonesian scholars who enriched my understanding about Indonesian society, namely Dr. Cecep Effendi, Dr. Makmur Keliat, Mr. Andy Rachmianto and Mr. Hariyadi Wirawan. I also express my profound sense of gratitude to my teacher, Prof. Parimal K. Das for his sharp comments and suggestions. I am beholden to Dr. M.M. Kaul, Amba Pandey, Pradeep Tandon and Gautam Jha in the division for their help. Prof. S.D. Muni, has been a source of inspiration and I am equally grateful to some Dutch scholars, especially Dr. Wim Stokhof, Director, IIAS, Leiden, for sharing their ideas and to all others who facilitated my work.

Finally, I express my appreciation and gratitude to Maulana Abul Kalam Azad Institute of Asian Studies, Calcutta, for appointing me a Project Fellow, and to International Institute of Asian Studies, Leiden, for offering me Affiliated Fellowship to facilitate this research. Lastly I owe my gratitude to Shipra Publishers who agreed to publish my book.

**Ganganath Jha**

# Contents

# 1

# Introduction

Indonesia situated at the crossroad of the Pacific and the Indian Ocean, is the largest country of Southeast Asia. It covers about 5,193,250 square kilometers of the territories, of which 2,027,087 sq. k.m. are landed and 3.166,163 sq. km. are sea territories. Again it is the largest archipelago of the world with 17,508 islands and 210 million population. Formerly under the Dutch colonial rule, it declared its independence on 17 August 1945 and became a Republic. Though the founding fathers tried to evolve a system in which all the three branches of the government, the executive, legislature and judiciary were to be equally vigilant, but Presidential system emerged and powers of the legislature and judiciary were eroded. First two Presidents, namely Sukarno (1945-65) and Suharto (1966-98) were extremely powerful and dominating. They increased the powers of the Presidency enormously and the mechanism of checks and balances were diluted. After getting independence, Indonesia tried to be assertive in the politics of the region in particular and Third World in general. President Sukarno was vocal against the western world and opposed US policy of containment. He endeavoured to nurture a system, which could prove ideal and indigenous by Asian standards. Thus the word Panchasila, also pronounced as Pancasila was popularised for the political system. Panchasila became the ideological and philosophical foundation of the Republic and its ideals were incorporated in the constitution declared on 18th August 1945.

Panchasila is a Sanskrit word, which was also considered the philosophical foundation of Indian Foreign Policy, but for India this word was incorporated in the document much later. Indonesia wanted to incorporate the ideals of Panchasila, both in foreign policy and domestic matters right since its inception. The Constitution of 1945 explained five principles of Panchasila as the following:[1]

- Belief in the one and only God.
- A just and civilised humanity.
- Unity of Indonesia.
- Democracy guided by the inner wisdom of deliberations of representatives.
- Social justice.

The Articles of the 1945 Constitution enumerated the ideals and goals for which the nation was born. The founding fathers were inspired by the urge for unity, common goals and democracy built upon the age-old Indonesian concepts of Gotong Royong (mutual assistance), of deliberations of representatives (Musya Warah) and consensus (Mufakat). Preceded by a preamble including Panchasila, the Constitution had 37 Articles defining the role of the Chief Executive (President), Legislature (MPR and DPR) and the Judiciary. The founding fathers envisaged the foundation of a unitary state with sovereignty vested in the legislature. However, the subsequent developments favoured the adoption of a Presidential system in which the President was very powerful. The President was projected as *primus interpares* and his council of ministers always looked to him for guidance and support. Both Sukarno and Suharto believed in the personality cult and strengthened the powers of the President enormously.

The sovereignty of the people was symbolised by Madjelis Permusjawaratan Rakjat (MPR), also known as people's consultative assembly. The number of members and the role of the members of the Dewan Perwakilan Rakjat (DPR) augmented with the representatives of the regions, political and Karja (functional) groups. The total number of appointed members to MPR was fixed at one third of the total number of MPR members and the number of MPR members were to be twice the total number of the members in DPR. Accordingly the members of the

MPR had been fixed at 1000 out of which 425 were elected, 75 appointed by the armed forces and the remaining 500 were government appointees.[2] MPR met every five years to elect and re-elect President and the latter was legally accountable to this House.

The legislative powers are in fact vested in the Dewan Perwakilan Rakjat (DPR) also known as the House of People's Representatives. According to 1969 Act, the number of members of DPR had been fixed at 460, of which 360 were elected and 100 nominated. However this figure was increased in 1975 to 500 of which 400 were elected and 100 were appointed members. Each member of the DPR pledged that they will always uphold the message of the people's sufferings, that they will adhere to and defend Panchasila as the basis and ideology of the state, the 1945 Constitution and all existing laws and regulations in force in the Republic of Indonesia, that they will endeavour to the best of their ability to promote the welfare of the Indonesian people and be loyal to the country, nation and the state of Indonesia.[3] They, however, proved a rubber stamp during 1965-99, but they started emerging as an important institution of rule making when Abdurrahman Wahid came into power.

The most striking feature of Indonesian politics is that it has not declared any state religion. Although the Muslims are in overwhelming majority and most of its neighbouring states have declared their state religion in order to maintain their national unity, Indonesia has abstained from doing so. Malaysia and Brunei, the two immediate neighbours, have declared Islam as the state religion but Indonesia preferred to remain secular. The preamble of 1945 Constitution assures religious freedom by declaring protection and promotion of faith in the God Almighty and endeavoured to create a just and civilised humanity. The various governments have been pursuing a religious policy, which respects the right of every religious groups and takes into account the feelings of all religious communities. They have officially recognised religions namely, Islam, Protestantism, Catholicism, Buddhism and Hinduism. As a result, there are

26,769 Protestant churches, 13,361 Catholic churches, 34408 Hindu temples, 2552 Buddhist *Viharas* and 537, 837 Muslim mosques.[4] The break up of the different religious communities in Indonesia in mid nineties indicated that Muslims comprised 87.2 per cent, Protestants 6 per cent, Catholics 3.5 per cent, Hindus 2 per cent and the Buddhists 1 per cent.[5]

Indonesia gives emphasis on "Unity in Diversity", to unite the people in a common fold. It has heterogeneous ethnic and linguistic groups. More than 300 languages are spoken and their culture and life style differ. The majority is of Malay stock, split into dozens of smaller sub groups, with varying family structures and social systems. The prominent ethnic groups are the Javanese, the Sundanese, the Minhasans, the Bugis, the Makassars and the Balinese. Again there are the Dayaks, the *Batak*s and *Dani* and the *Asmat* of Melanesian stock.

There is sufficient impact of Sufism on art and culture, namely the *Wayang*, myths and folklores, poems and songs, the Islamic calendar, ceremonies and festivals, etc. Sufi saints understood that Javanese were very fond of art, so they inserted Islamic teachings in the stories of *Ramayana* and *Mahabharata* to be played in *Wayang*. They created new myths, stories, poems and songs, which had local names, local languages but Islamic teachings. A Sufi saint, Walisongo led the Sufi movement in the 15th century and became very popular in Java with Islamic ideologies. His strategy of adopting local stories, local heroes and myths were adopted by the Sufi saints in other parts of the archipelago.

## Threats to the Republic

Indonesia is faced with numerous problems of different types but here an attempt is made to point out outstanding political problems. The archipelagic concept as enunciated by the founding fathers are losing its importance and Panchasila doctrine, especially its third principle "Unity of Indonesia" has been endangered. The separatist movement in Aceh and Irian Jaya are too serious to be ignored. East Timor which had been annexed after a military action in 1975 has already become an independent State in 1999, and similar demands are articulated by separatists in Aceh and Irian Jaya.

Aceh, situated at the northernmost region of Sumatra, have a distinct culture and history. Its 4.5 million population has been strong supporter of *Darul* Islam movement and views the authority of Central government un-Islamic. This is because the government is dominated by Javanese, who are *Abangans*. The people of Aceh has been struggling for its own identity and separate nationhood because the government of Indonesia has not been sensitive to their grievances. The government gave them autonomy in religious and educational affairs after a long struggle in 1959 but it was withdrawn without any rhyme or reason. Though it is rich in iron, oil, gas and coal, it is not given any share in the benefits. At the same time, the government has supported migration and transmigration of population to that area which has been disliked. The people in Aceh have opposed the presence of new migrants and they have been agitating. The continuing conflicts over economic and demographic issues have fuelled separatist movement. In 1976, *Hasan Di Tiro* established *Gerakan* Aceh *Merdeka* (Free Aceh movement) and subsequently declared independence. But this movement was suppressed and Tiro fled to Sweden. It was from Sweden that he announced the formation of Aceh government in exile. The unrest mounted enormously in Aceh in 1989 when National Liberation Front Aceh Sumatra (NLFAS) was established. They mounted onslaughts on the government forces and Amnesty International claimed that 2000 people were killed during 1989-93, and the casualty number have been increasing every year.

Similar is the situation in Irian Jaya, where Organisasi Papua Merdeka (OPM), also known as Free Papua movement leads separatist movement. There has been lot of bloodshed in that province also and the cases of human rights violations are reported. Irian Jaya is rich in timber, gold and silver. Indonesia is trying to exploit the natural resources of the area, but the indigenous people are resisting it. They have not yet been fully integrated with the national mainstream as their outlook and culture are different. They have not accepted their integration so far and they display much in common with the people of Papua New Guinea. It is a fact that Dani, Asmat and other ethnic groups of the province are of Melanesian stock and they are entirely different in their customs and traditions compared to Javanese Malays. Some of the tribal groups have procured weapons to kill transmigrants and foreigners. The army, on the other hand, has been vindictive while assuring law and order.

The separatist tendencies in both Aceh and Irian Jaya have religious dimension. As far as Aceh is concerned, it is Muslim dominated area. They believe that the government of Indonesia is under the control of the Javanese, and a Javanese cannot be a true Muslim. The Javanese leaders have reciprocated such a feeling regarding the nationalism of Acehnese as well. There has been persecution of the leaders in Aceh and mass graves have been found. Some of the dissident leaders have left their homeland to seek asylum elsewhere. Their participation in the government has been nominal and guerrilla warfare continues. On the other hand, Irian Jaya has 83 per cent Christian population. The Church is the main centre of social congregation. They know that the province had not been handed over to Indonesia along with other provinces by the Dutch colonial masters on ethnic and religious grounds. Their projection is that given the situation in which they are, their identity is bound to be lost forever in Indonesian state.

The socio-economic factor is the root cause of trouble in Ambon also. History says that majority of the pro-Dutch elements and militias inhabited in that area especially on the eve of independence. They had struggled against their integration with the Indonesian Republic and had fought for their independence. Known as Amboina in the historical past, Ambon has a number of people with Dutch descent. There are some people with Portuguese origin. On the other hand, there are some Chinese traders, who have prospered in business and trade. Although the government statistics claim that 55.8 per cent are Muslims, 38.2 per cent are Protestants and 5.3 per cent are

Catholics, but this figure needs to be verified. A study of social life in Ambon shows that it is a Christian dominated area. There is disparity in the life style of the Muslims and Christians. Catholic Christians are relatively better economically than their Muslim counterparts.

There has been violent clashes between the Muslims and Christian communities especially after Indonesia was gripped by the economic crisis (1997-98). Hundreds of people have lost their lives. Militant groups have emerged to protect the lives of their people and communal virus has engulfed the area. Islamic outfits such as Islamic Defender's Forum have given a call for *Jehad* and such a call is appropriately reciprocated. It is believed that the government was lackadaisical in their attitudes about the happenings in the area in the post 1998 period and did not act swiftly to stop rioting.

The development in Aceh, Irian Jaya, and Ambon clearly suggest that the concept of *Bhineka Tunggal Eka* (Unity in Diversity) is endangered. We find that there are growing threats to minorities. The Chinese for instance have felt traumatic experiences. Anti-Chinese riots have taken place in Jakarta also on one pretext or the other.

The ethnic Chinese are feeling threatened in all parts of the country. The Chinese, who have traditionally been involved in business and trade, and who have prospered economically are made victims of looting, arson, rape, riots and humiliation ever since the beginning of *Habibie* era in 1998. Anti-Chinese riots have been taking place and the worst affected areas are Medan, Titipatan, Solo and Samarinda. The hooligans involved in rioting argue that the Chinese are responsible for spiralling price rise and the economic crisis. In February 1998, the riots in Medan were serious enough to compel some ethnic Chinese to leave their houses. Twelve Chinese owned shops had been torched and dozens of buildings damaged at Kendari in Sulawesi. The looting of Chinese stores and shops have been occurring ever since.[6]

Again the Communal life has been tense ever since religion and ethnicity were used as weapons in politics. President

Suharto, who had secular credentials ever since he came into power, felt the need to establish *Ikatan Cendekiawan Muslim* Indonesia (ICMI) in December 1990. Though B.J. Habibie is given credits for establishing this ICMI, but in reality it was born with the support of Suharto. The ICMI objectives were to face the challenges of the Islamic parties and provide ideological and philosophical support to Panchasila democracy. It was made essential for every Islamic academics and intellectuals to be a member of ICMI and work for it. As a result, other religious groups also started activating their associations and the problems started complicating with the dawn of Habibie era (1998-99). The Christians were targeted by the Muslims and they are not feeling safe as riots have taken place against them at Ambon and other cities. The *loompens* are let loose with the tacit support of the Islamic fanatics.

Again the religion had come in the path of *Megawati Sukarnoputri's* candidature as President of Indonesia. Though she is a popular leader and daughter of Sukarno the Father of the Nation, her credentials to uphold Muslim values are questioned because of her genealogy. When her candidature for Presidency was considered, there were lots of debates that her mother and grandmother were Hindus and therefore her Muslim heritage is diluted. The military supported Golkar Party made allegation that *Megawati* was secretly praying at a Hindu temple in Bali. Another criticism was that she had chosen a majority of non-Muslim Candidates for her party, and if appointed the President, her conduct would be identical. Finally since she is a woman, she can't be appointed the head of State of a Muslim dominated country. All these opinions prevailed in the deliberations of the MPR in 1999. Though Abdurrahman Wahid had won only 54 seats compared to 153 of *Megawati Sukarnoputri*, but his support grew rapidly in MPR. Besides other factors, religion played significant role in mobilising support for him. He got 373 votes in the race for Presidency, whereas *Megawati* secured only 313. The result was so surprising that the demand for directly elected President on the pattern of the U.S. in Indonesia had been mooted.

Needless to say that religion is assuming center stage and the use of Islam is increasing in the struggle for power. Nahdlatul *Ulama* (NU), Muhammadiah and Syarikat Islam (IS) have a feeling that they would lose their popular support if they ignore importance of Islamic religion in socio-economic life. They may be right that Islam is the single most important factor in the unity of the community, but overemphasis is counterproductive as Indonesia has multi-ethnic and multi-religious society. If the religion is used for power politics, it can generate forces of destabilisation and disintegration and this logic is particularly relevant in Indian and Indonesian context. *Darul* Islam in Indonesia, for instance, has been advocating *Jehad*, Islamic purity, and violence. They are influential in Aceh and the result is social tension which is disastrous. Indonesia indeed has been facing challenges through religious groups but its beginning can be traced ever since its independence. Masjumi Party (*Majlis Sura Muslim Indonesia*) influenced by the teachings of Mohammed Abduh of Cairo University, which had mobilised support of the Muslims in Sumatra, South Sulawesi and West Java, was highly critical of Marxist oriented socialism of Sukarno. It had posed serious problems to Sukarno administration, particularly when guided democracy was declared. Masjumi leaders argued that a renewed Islam was capable of providing a religious and philosophical base for rapid social and economic development. It believed in replacing Panchasila-based Indonesia to one founded on Islam. Mohammed Natsir, a Masjumi leader pleaded that since Islam was the religion and philosophy of most Indonesians, the Islamic majority should not accept a state based on secular Panchasila, because secularism is an alien concept. This Party was advocating the inclusion of *Shariat* laws in the constitution and their activities created serious problems for Sukarno administration. Hence his government moved to ban this organisation. Though this party was officially banned, its appeal continued to exist.

In fact, the role of religious groups and missionaries cannot be overlooked in the context of Indonesia because of their constructive role in the freedom struggle. It was *Hajis* (visiting Mecca on pilgrimage) who worked for anti-colonial struggle. Whenever they returned after their pilgrimage, they felt the need of indigenous, Islamic political order, purification and even outright assertion against the colonial masters. They began to express their critical views about the political system. They began to evaluate and review the role of their social and religious institutions which helped the colonial rulers to perpetuate their rule. It was common for *Hajis* and their circle of followers to express critical views about *Adat*, (customs and traditions of Islam) which were making them subservient to the colonial rulers. One of them, named Haji Muhammad Rifangi who led Buduah movement among the rural population of Pekalongan and Kedari advocated religious reforms. He tried to mobilise public opinion to boycott official rituals in the Kalisalak mosque. The Dutch colonial government was annoyed so much so that Rifangi was exiled to Maluku.

Another *Haji* who became a national figure was Haji Abdul Karim of Banten. He established a Pesantren School in Banten and tried to evolve Islamic Political thinking. He travelled throughout Banten holding purification rights, *Ziki* and holy processions. He was regarded very devout possessing divine powers. He was one of the first, who had predicted inevitability of *Jehad* (holy war) for the survival of Islam, the arrival of Mahdi and subsequently the ushering of a new era.[7]

*Hajis* had always played significant role in the nationalist upsurge. Whether it was Boedi Oetomo or *Sarekat* Islam, they were born with the support and insight of the *Hajis*. Boedi Oetomo established by Indonesian intellectuals in 1908 for educational purposes, started working for political consciousness. Subsequently *Sarekat* Islam was born in 1912 under the leadership of *Haji* Samanhudi. Though the apparent objective of *Sarekat* Islam was to strengthen business relations with the Dutch empire, it turned out to be a political party under the leadership of H.O.S. Tjokroaminoto, Haji Agoes Salim and others. *Hajis* had played significant role in the establishment of Muhammadiah also in the same year under the leadership of K.H. Ahmad Dahlan in Jogyakarta. Again Partai Indonesia was formed by Setiabudi, Tjipto Mangunkusumo and K.I. Hajar Dewantoro in the same year.

The religious groups in Aceh made great contributions in the freedom struggle and the pursuit of revolution against the colonial masters. The Pesantren and the Ulemas mobilised training centres for freedom fighters.[8] One of the famous leaders of Aceh was Tengku Cik Tiro, who contributed new insights in the nationalist upsurge by advocating that the Dutch psyche understands the language of violence and war only. The negotiations and dialogues are redundant to gain nationalist goals. Tiro was educated and trained in Pesantren. He advocated self-rule for the Indonesians and was extremely critical of the Dutch colonial system. He argued that the Dutch regime was exploitative and opposed to Islamic ideas. He established links with reformist Muslims and anti-colonial forces in Java to arouse anti-Dutch sentiments. His followers in Aceh had taken up arms to fight battles against the Dutch colonial forces. Tiro propagated guerrilla warfare and preferred jungles and mountains to confront the enemy. He was successful in igniting the nationalist forces and intermittent warfare became the outcome of his efforts in Aceh.

The followers of Tiro preached that the blessings of the Allah are unlimited for those who serve for the community and fight for the Muslim nation. All those who are ready to serve and sacrifice, are dear to the Allah, who gives name, fame and wealth to dear and devouts. He blesses paradise full of lights to martyrs. Their appeals had long-term implications. The Dutch colonial forces were unable to cope with the challenges, but independence in 1945 did not bring an Islamic state. The new rulers thought that unity of the country was more important and accepting Islam as state religion would have adverse reactions on Christian dominated areas.

In short, it can be stated that the interplay of religion with society is key to understanding Indonesian politics. Japanese invaders knew this and nurtured the activities of Islamic institutions to neutralise the Dutch interference. Islamic leaders were anti-Dutch in their activities and temperament and therefore they supported the Japanese as friends to throw out the Dutch colonial rulers. Sukarno, the father of the nation, however was not in favour of establishing an Islamic state. He astutely manoeuvred the support of the members in the Constituent Assembly to dilute this proposal. He stimulated his people to evolve other revolutionary ideas while assuring that he will protect religious interests of the Indonesian people. Panchasila became the preamble of the 1945 constitution and equal status was offered to five religions. Muslim clergies who continued to grumble disliked this.

Though the downfall of Sukarno is attributed to several factors but one of them was the opposition of important Islamic groups. They were critical of his socialist rhetorics, land reforms and dependence on communist forces. His successor, General Suharto initially cultivated the Islamic religious groups and indulged in *Jehad* of the communists, but did not do anything to alter the constitution to suit their demands. The Muslim groups remained suppressed and ultimately felt cheated. They gradually started supporting Nahdlatul Ulama and Muhammadiyah to fulfil their interests. These organisations subsequently became vocal critics of the Suharto regime, which forced Suharto to counter them at the intellectual level. He thus supported his information and technology Minister, B.J. Habibie to float ICMI (Ikatan Cendikiawan Muslim Indonesia) in 1990.

ICMI stands for improvements in all aspects of life. Habibie said: "ICMI is not a political organisation. Its main objective is to make a real contribution to ever-increasing challenges to the way of life of the whole Indonesian population, especially the Islamic community".[9] Notwithstanding the government patronage, ICMI became controversial. The main Muslim organisations viewed it as an instrument of the government, bent on relieving the role of

Islam in Indonesian politics.[10] They proved right and subsequently when Suharto resigned in 1998, ICMI lost its appeal. However, the reality is that Suharto felt the need to cultivate religious groups in order to survive politically which underlines the importance of religion in contemporary politics of Indonesia.

Abdurrahman Wahid's selection as Presidential candidate at the cost of Megawati was inspired by religious groups. Though a product of Pesantren and innovative, Wahid as a politician could not deal with serious challenges posed to him by some other religious groups. The situation in Aceh and Irian Jaya are disturbing where the separatist movement is mainly based on religious and economic grounds. East Timor became independent because differences between Islam and Christianity remained unabridged. Religion is an important weapon available to political parties and if it can get the support of religious leaders and the innovators of mysticism, it can prove deadly. Though Wahid excelled in strategy, mission and vision, the paradigm of power politics generated unpredictable forces. He could not stand trial for corruption charges. He was forced to resign and Megawati Sukarnoputri was appointed the President. As the daughter of Sukarno and an activist for democracy movement, she has secular credentials. Her predicament is to balance her politics regarding the Armed Forces, Islamic and Christian associations and her own followers in order to survive and provide example of good governance and stability. Growth rates are to be accelerated and transparency in administrative decisions are to be displayed.

Indonesia is on the democratic path and it is not easy to harmonise religion with development, order and secularism to the satisfaction of all its citizens. It is a fact that Indonesians believe in mysticism and nobody can stop its impact at the community level. How it will evolve and affect the system, the leadership and broader politics are unpredictable. However, it is important to give vent to the grievances of the people necessary for the stability and prosperity of the nation.

The leaders of the present order have to review the role of the Armed Forces in the politics of the country. Their intrusion in administration and politics had been legitimated with the acceptance of *dwifungsi* (Dual Functions)[11]. The meaning and significance of *dwifungsi* were aimed at perpetrating army rule. It was argued that the concern of the armed forces were not simply to look after national defence, but also the actual conduct of the government in the interest of good administration. A powerful propaganda was made that the armed forces had played the principal role in securing independence, that it had done so in the face of obstruction and betrayal by the civilian authorities, and it therefore retained a special right and duty to supervise and take charge of the government. Under the stewardship of Suharto, *dwifungsi* principle became operational and accordingly serving and retired army officers took a wide variety of posts, from that of a cabinet minister down to a village head.

Though the leading role of the army in the freedom struggle is a historical reality, but the fact that it played some negative role subsequently, cannot be overlooked. They had assumed a major role in the economy as the managers of the Dutch enterprises, which had been nationalised in 1957. They took major part in the administrative system and their performances were not satisfactory. They did their best to suppress democratic ethos, which had been cultivated at the time of freedom struggle. The increasing importance of *dwifungsi* resulted in turning democratic institutions subservient to promote army rule and thus political parties, pressure groups, media and information channels had limited freedom to express their viewpoints. The number of appointed members grew enormously in the House of Representatives (DPR) and the MPR (People's Consultative Assembly) was made almost redundant. MPR used to be convened at the end of every five years to appoint a President, whose candidature were decided by the armed forces. The legislature was treated as a rubber stamp and it was difficult to speak anything against omission and commission of the officials. The intelligence network to monitor the activities of the civilian population were outrageous and Indonesians could reflect their opinions about their political system only after much persuasion. But when they realised that restoration of democracy is imminent, they began to articulate their viewpoints.

When Suharto resigned on 21 May 1998, there were jubilation, but it ushered into an era of political uncertainty and instability. Even though democracy was restored, anarchic situation prevailed. The ethnic disputes erupted and riots abetted. The violence, riots and vandalism at Aceh, Ambon and Irian Jaya as highlighted to the outside world through internet and media are reprehensible. The democratic leaders have to perform their tasks more astutely and prove their management skills. The armed forces should not feel neglected at the same time. They exercise enormous clout in the socio-economic life and command prestige. They have vested interests in politics and economics. The leaders in the present government have to be highly sensitive to their opinion, without which the task of nation building, stability and development cannot be promoted. Instituting inquiry committees, special courts and open hearings against the armed forces might not yield the desired results. The special investigation implicating some Generals in East Timor massacres proved to be contentious. The report assumed political colour when the name of General Wironto was mentioned. It was a pretext to demand the resignation of the General from the cabinet and he had no choice but to resign. In retrospect, it was found that the conviction was not convincing. General Wironto was honest and widely respected and his ouster had been disliked by a section of the people and the armed forces. If the armed forces are offended, it can prove very costly for evolving democratic experiments.

Indonesia is also known for corruption and cronyism in high places. Former President Suharto supported his children to develop business connections, based on privileged access to government contracts, licenses and subsidies. Hutomo Putra Mandala (Tommy) had obtained exclusive rights for the purchase of cloves from farmers. He extracted benefits from monopolies over flour and tin plates. He also got the coveted authorisation to produce Indonesian car (*Pt Timor Putra Nasional*) and establish Sempati Air. Suharto's daughter, Siti Prabowo got the share in a $ 10 billion project linking Malaysia and Indonesia over the Malacca Straits. Likewise his two other sons Bambang and Sigit Harjojudanto had greatly benefited in business matters because of their genealogy and the President knew it. The Economist (London) had reported that the members of the Suharto clan could walk into any State Bank and demand a loan at favourable terms. The government always awarded the juicy contracts to Suharto family in the areas of power generation, telecommunications and toll-roads.[12] The corruption and cronyism had become an important part of his administration and the socio-economic life had started feeling too much pressure. The political and economic situation had deteriorated because most of the monitoring agencies—the legislature and judiciary—had become subservient to the executive. The political parties were either banned or if they survived they had to observe a code of conduct favourable to the armed forces. They had to express their faith in Panchasila, which had been declared a national ideology, which was treated sacred for every Indonesian.[13] The Suharto regime was named Panchasila democracy and the government was responsible for formulation of ideas and interpretation of the Panchasila. The meaning of Panchasila had been stretched too far aimed at prescribing a society modelled on the traditional family, in which parental authority was respected and in which individual interest was subordinate to the community. The government came forward with some laws under its framework like Panchasila labor relations, which implied that there could be no conflict of interest between workers and management and that the strikes were inherently anti-social. The dissent or opposition to the dictates of the government was not allowed. The Presidency had assumed all the powers of the government advertently or inadvertently, and under the system the maxim that "power corrupts and absolute power corrupts absolutely" became a reality.

Political reform has been on the agenda of the government in the post-Suharto era. They have decided to lift control over the political parties and thus multi-party system have emerged. All parties are given financial aid from the government and the amount depends on the number of votes received in the elections.[14] They also want to activate MPR and DPR by reducing the number of appointed members and increasing their powers in rule making. For instance, although the MPR was declared supreme power through article I of the 1945 Constitution, vested with three important tasks, namely approving the constitution, deciding the guidelines of state policy and election of the President and Vice-President, its authority has been eroded. It was authorised to convene a special session whenever necessary but it met only once in five years. MPR indeed had abdicated all its responsibilities except ritually appointing the President after five years. Now there is a growing demand that it should play an active role in decision making. The first step in that direction has been the reduction in the numbers of appointed members and according to 1999 Act of the government, the members of the MPR are reduced to 700 only, instead of 1000. However, the most important aspect of the reform process is that they have decided to restore Article 28 of the 1945 constitution in letter and spirit, which guarantees "the right of free assembly and association, of expression of opinion, orally or in writing" to the Indonesian citizens.

## Human Rights

The issues concerning human rights of Indonesian people have assumed importance as it is an important element of civilised society. It has been suppressed in many countries of the Third World and Indonesia is no exception. It has assumed significance in the New World Order as the United States is the ardent advocate of assuring it at the universal level. Though the United Nations General Assembly proclaimed the Universal Declaration of Human Rights in 1948 itself and emphasised that all human beings are born free and equal in dignity and rights, and endowed with reason and conscience, and should act towards one another in a spirit of brotherhood, this has been ignored very often in course of drives for nation building and modernisation. Indonesia has signed the covenants for the Universal Declaration but it has been found lacking in implementing it. Amnesty International published "Indonesia: Shock Therapy Restoring Order in Aceh: 1989-93", and revealed many cases of omission and commission committed by the government. Similarly, there were numerous reports about excesses committed in East Timor, which broke away from Indonesia in 1999. If we go into the genesis of the conflict, we find logic on both sides.

Indonesia gave priority to economic development in the era of new order (1965-98) and that was in tune with international covenant on economic, social and cultural rights (*Unga Resolution 2200*). In accordance with the Universal Declaration of Human Rights, the ideal law of free human beings, enjoying freedom from fear and want, can only be achieved if the conditions are created whereby everyone may enjoy his economic, social and cultural rights, as well as his civil and political rights. The removal of poverty is essential in order to promote human rights. Indonesia adopted development programmes for its impoverished population in 1967, when Suharto signed the documents of declaration of world leaders on population. In view of this policy, national family planning programmes were supported and the schemes proved successful in limiting the increase of population, which are below 3 million population growth annually. Total fertility rate came down to 50 per cent as desired by the government and Indonesian expertise was appreciated in most of the neighbouring countries. But the policy, which proved controversial, was regarding transmigration of the people from densely populated areas to less populated zones.

Java and Bali inhabit 65 per cent of Indonesian population. Java alone has 100 million people. This island however occupies only 6.8 per cent of the total land of the country. Sumatra, which is comparatively bigger in size, has 41 million, Sulawesi 13 million, Nusatenggara 11.5 million, Maluku 11.9 million and

Kalimantan has 11 million population.[15] It is known that only 992 out of 17508 islands are mainly populated zones. But Haryati Scebadio says that 5000 islands are inhabited.[16] There has to be a better management of the inhabited and uninhabited islands to accelerate the pace of development. There is abundance of natural resources in all parts of the country and their exploitation can be facilitated only when there is availability of manpower. Indonesia endeavoured to diversify its population from densely populated areas to new zones. They passed relevant rules in that direction in 1960 and 1973 and transmigrated people from Java to other islands. Initially, 17116 families were settled in Irian Jaya and 8155 in Maluku but a number of people were also transmigrated to Kalimantan, East Timor and Aceh.[17] Joan Hardejono said that the number of transmigration were 49772 in 1979-80, 108081 in 1980-81, 123846 in 1981-82, 167477 in 1982-83 and 86298 in 1983-84.[18] As the government supported it, transmigration continued but it has not resolved the problem of population density in Java. As job opportunities are available mostly in Java, poor and impoverished people continue to come and the problem remains the same.

There has been some omission and commission, while transmigrating the people as alleged by Aceh Merdeka, OPM and some other opposition groups. They stated that the alien population is arbitrarily introduced to change the demographic complexion and this is a matter of intrusion in matters of their human rights. They understand that the transmigrantes would alter the indigenous character of their socio-economic life and usurp their properties. The Javanese speak an alien language and have faith in Islamic religion. But the people in Irian Jaya and Ambon have significant number of Christians. The indigenous people are unhappy that their distinct identity would be diluted in due course if the arrival of transmigrantes are not stopped. They allege that Javanese migrants are arrogant with a sense of superiority. They assume that they are unwanted people thrust upon them, who may be interested in colonising the entire area. The new migrants generally search jobs in oil exploration, mining and forestry department and the local people project this behaviour contrary to their interests saying that ultimately the new transmigrantes would deprive them of their resources and wealth.[19]

Indigenous people in Irian Jaya, Aceh and Ambon are alarmed by the activities of the ethnic Javanese. They observe that the Javanese migrants have excellent rapport with government authorities. They are trusted by the government and offered all types of facilities at the cost of the indigenous people. Hence, they are demanding that the transmigration should be scrapped with immediate effect. Thus transmigrant population are faced with a dilemma in coping with the situation and the human rights of transmigrated have been threatened. The opposition to government policies remained suppressed under the authoritarian rule, but now the situation is changing very fast. Although transmigration has been stopped, the present government has to cope with the challenges of transmigration policies of Suharto era. With restoration of democracy, it is natural that the issue of transmigration is politicised and it would be more complicated in due course.

It may prove more suitable and less controversial if the transmigration is directed towards those islands where there are no population at all and such areas as assessed by the government sources are more than two thirds of the inhabited islands. The people might not be interested in inhabiting in new areas because of poor living conditions and necessary infrastructure, but the government should take the assistance of the international financial institutions to create necessary conditions for settlement on uninhabited islands of Indonesia.

Besides human rights, the issue of environment have assumed importance in Indonesia in the past few years. The increasing denudation of forests and logging have to be stopped completely. The forest fires creating smoky haze have to be contained. But Indonesia has the shortage of fire fighting machines. It was due to this that the forest fire in Sumatra and Borneo in 1997 engulfed a large part of Southeast Asia for months. The fire had reached Malaysia, Brunei, Singapore and Australia as well. The smoky haze generated a number of health problems and disrupted tourism and transport systems. A forest fire at Sumatra in March 1999 caught Malaysia and Singapore as well. The neighbouring countries are alarmed by the recurring forest fire in Indonesia. These developments have grave implications on Indonesian image outside, and therefore the government has to evolve a sound policy to check fire in its jungles and co-operate more closely with the ASEAN regional task force to monitor and put stop to it.

Although environmental problems are serious, they can be resolved with the support of the ASEAN, the APEC and the UN. What is more difficult and complicated is to maintain territorial integrity of Indonesia. The independence of East Timor has opened floodgates for disintegration. There is separatist movements in Aceh, Irian Jaya and Ambon. The Christians are unhappy with their Islamic counterparts. The terrorist groups have emerged to protect their ethnic groups. Islamic outfits are clamouring for *Jehad* and similarly the Christians have taken up arms in vengeance and there is bloodshed. Although Aceh is intra-Muslim conflict, Irian Jaya and Ambon present a different scenario. In both these cases, the conflict is between two religious groups, *i.e.* Muslims and Christians. There is a history behind these conflicts which cannot be overlooked. The Ambonese in Maluku had embarked on separation on the eve of independence of the Indonesian Republic. On 25 April 1950, Ambonese leaders, J.H. Manuhuttu and A. Wairisai had proclaimed the establishment of the state of South Moluccas. Indonesian government felt great concern, but projected the conflict as a family quarrel.[20] But when the Ambonese, who had served in the Dutch army, started fighting against the government, the separatists took the control of Ambon and adjoining islands, and it was not easy for the government to resolve this problem for quite some time. The government had to organise sea blockade by the Indonesian navy to contain dissident activities. As Ambon is dependent on other islands for its food supply, the sea blockade crippled them. It was only thereafter that troops were dispatched to take control of Ambon and adjoining islands. Ambonese leaders did not give up their idea of independence even after the defeat. Some of them fled to Holland and continued to oppose their integration with Indonesia.

The history of Irian Jaya is more or less similar. The Dutch government had retained it while transferring sovereignty of other islands to Indonesian leaders. The Dutch colonial masters viewed that Irian Jaya was much different in culture, religion and ethnicity to be integrated in Indonesia. Another dimension of the Dutch policy was to create a homeland for the people of Dutch - Indonesian descent on that island, where a sizeable section of the indigenous people opposed their integration with Indonesia.[21] The government of Indonesia, on the other hand, invoked the principle of archipelagic concept and fought for the control of the island. Irian Jaya became a part of Indonesia only after the intervention of the United Nations in 1963 but it continued to remain isolated and backward. When East Timor became independent in 1999, it had its impact on political developments in Irian Jaya as well. What is striking is that the church and the Christian associations have played important role in the freedom struggle of East Timor. Hence the role of Christian institutions and associations are gaining new meaning in the context of Irian Jaya and Ambon and counter developments are taking place. It is a matter of concern that Islamic groups are alarmed and advocate *Jehad* for an Islamic state. The development activities are opposed by the natives. If there is logging or mining, it is resisted by the separatists on various grounds. The separatist leaders argue that their natural resources are exploited for the benefit of the Javanese and they cannot get justice under the present dispensation. The Armed Forces, which ruled the country from 1965 to 1998, have committed atrocities and suppressed dissidents. Now that democracy has dawned, they have started articulating their grievances in public. It demands lot of courage and wisdom to involve them in the decision making and make them feel secure as distinct ethnic groups in their respective areas. The principle of "unity in diversity" has to be implemented in letter and spirit, and ethnic leaders are to be promoted in national decision making

To conclude, it can be stated that the problem of national integration is complicated and there is threat to unity of Indonesia. Irian Jaya, Aceh and Ambon are disturbed and solution to their grievances are not in sight. Although the dissidents would welcome referendum on the pattern in East Timor, it is difficult now. When Habibie had announced referendum, it was without taking the consent of the DPR, which is the supreme decision making body. His successor, Wahid also announced referendum for Aceh without discussing it in the DPR, which is the proper forum where such resolutions should first be discussed. Naturally there was immediate opposition to the proposal, and when the issue was referred to DPR it was opposed. The representatives of the people in the Assembly rejected Wahid's proposals and established an expert panel to suggest measures to resolve the dispute. In December 1999, the expert panel on Aceh recommended policy alternatives, which did not include a referendum on Acehnese independence.[22] It is known that the secession of any one province would encourage fragmentation of the Indonesian republic resulting in political instability in the region. The Indonesian legislature (DPR) might be ready to discuss autonomy proposals. For instance, DPR representatives are suggesting that Aceh might be allowed to decree radical Islamic Laws in place of Panchasila. It may be apportioned up to 75 per cent of the revenues on account of its oil, besides the right to generate other sources of revenues.[23] Similarly Irian Jaya, which is the largest and remotest province of Indonesia, can think about autonomy. The DPR might discuss apportioning the share of that province in the profits due to mining of gold, logging of timber, etc. They may be allowed to declare Christian laws, but the secession of the province cannot be entertained.

To sum up, there are some issues which demand immediate attention. First, Article 1 of the 1945 constitution states that "sovereignty is vested in the people to be fully exercised by the elected MPR vested with supreme power". This house is meant to voice the social and political aspirations of the people and the President is made accountable to it. However its powers were eroded and it was summoned for ceremonial occasions only. It was convened only after the gap of five years to elect a new President. Thus it became a rubber stamp under the stewardship of Sukarno and Suharto. The role of the MPR has to be reviewed in the light of political developments since 1945 so that it is enabled to check and balance the political system. The President should be compelled to feel accountable to it and there should no dilution of the separation of powers of the three branches of the government as enunciated in the constitution.

Secondly, the ideals of Panchasila although became the philosophical foundation of the Indonesian republic, it became very controversial during the stewardship of President Suharto. When Sukarno was overthrown and Suharto assumed control of the political power on 11 March 1966, the latter period was projected as ushering into an era of Panchasila democracy. In fact, the military dictatorship under which millions of PKI supporters were killed, *dwifungsi* was evolved and opposition suppressed, Suharto took the support of Panchasila to legitimize his actions. Hence trade unions faced restrictions in the name of Panchasila and political parties were suppressed in the name of Panchasila. A situation developed in which Panchasila became synonymous with military dictatorship. Hence the elan of Panchasila for unification of the country was lost. Indonesia, being multi-ethnic and multi-religious, have to search a new symbol and concept which can substitute Panchasila to maintain the unity and solidarity of the nation. The archipelagic concept has to be reinforced in conjunction with Panchasila philosophy to promote integrationist forces.

Finally, although democracy has dawned, authoritarianism has prevailed in Indonesia for centuries. Whether in Dutch or post-Dutch political order, the opposition to the establishment has not been tolerated. President Sukarno started with democracy but ended with crushing it with an iron hand. Suharto presided over a military rule and so there was less scope for dissent and discussion. The cultural ethos is to obey and not to question the wisdom of the leaders. However, democracy is the only form of government, in which aspirations of the people can be fulfilled and unity and solidarity of the people can be enhanced to the satisfaction of the majority. Nevertheless the threat of authoritarian rule cannot be ruled out if there is continued threat to the unity of the country by the dissident groups. The turmoil and instability in Indonesia generates grave implications for geo-politics of the region. Whatever happened in East Timor, have been reverberating on the security environment of Irian Jaya, Mindanao and Kashmir. If constitutional means prove ineffective, authoritarianism is bound to evolve.

## Reference


1. Indonesia (1997) An Official Handbook, Jakarta Department of Information, Republic of Indonesia, pp.37-40.
2. The Composition and the Status of the MPR, DPR and Regional House of Representatives, Jakarta, Department of Information, Republic of Indonesia, 1996, pp. 9-10.
3. Ibid., pp 19-20.
4. Indonesia Handbook, Jakarta, Department of Information, 1989, pp.196.
5. Indonesia, Information Section, Embassy of the Republic of Indonesia, New Delhi, 1995, p.64.
6. The Times of India, New Delhi, 20 February 1998.
7. For details, see, Zuhri, K.H.Saifuddin, The History of Islamic Resurgence and Development in Indonesia, Bandung, 1979.
8. For better analysis of this aspect see Noer Deliar, The Modernist Muslim Movement in Indonesia, 1900-1942, Kuala Lumpur 1973.
9. Adam Schwartz, A Nation in Waiting, Indonesia in the 1990s, Melbourne, 1994, p.179.
10. *Ibid.*
11. General Edi Sudradjat, "The Dual Function of the Indonesian Armed Forces", Indonesia, New Delhi, Embassy of the Republic of Indonesia, 1995, p.32, and also see Nrugroho Notosusanto, The National Struggle and the Armed Forces in Indonesia, Jakarta, Department of Defence and Security 1982.
12. "Indonesia: Dear Daddy", The Economist, 13-19 December 1997, p.61.

13. "Panchasila, the State Philosophy", Indonesia: An Official Handbook, Jakarta, Department of Information, 1997, 0.41.
14. "Political Reform", Image of Indonesia, Jakarta, July 1998, p.3.
15. Juwono Sudarsono, "The Challenges to Indonesia's Unity", Indonesia: 50 Years, Embassy of the Republic of Indonesia, New Delhi, 1995, p.51.
16. Haryati Soebadio, ed., Dynamics of Indonesian History, Amstardam, North Holland Publishing Company, 1978 preface.
17. Soewartoyo, "Internal Migration between Java - Bali and Eastern Indonesia", Indonesia Quarterly, Vol.24, No.3, 1996, p.130.
18. Joan Hardjono, "Transmigration: Looking to the Future", Bulletin of Indonesian Economics Studies, Vol.22, No.2, August 1986, p.29.
19. Michael Richardson, "Making Irian Jaya Pay its Way", Far Eastern Economic Review, 13 June 1975, p.15.
20. Harja W. Bachtiar, The Indonesia Nation: Some Problems of Integration and Disintegration, Singapore ISEAS, 1976, pp.29-30.
21. *Ibid.*, p.31.
22. P.S. Suryanarayana, "Wahid talks tough on Aceh", Hindu, 5 December 1999.
23. Hindu, 28 November 1999.

## 2

# Indonesian Society

The population of Indonesia is the fourth largest in the world after China, India and the United States. According to latest estimates the total population is 210 million. The growth rate of the population has been 2.32 per cent and the attempts are made to reduce the birth rates. Indonesia has more than 17508 islands but only 6000 of them are inhabited.[1] Situated at the crossroad of the two oceans, the Pacific Ocean and the Indian Ocean, the country is very important geo-strategically. It is the largest country of Southeast Asia, and covers almost half the territories of the region. Malacca, Lombok and Sunda Straits are important sealanes and this is the largest oil exporting country in the region.

Indonesian archipelago is divided into three groups. The islands of Java, Sumatra and Kalimantan with the smaller islands in between lie on the Sunda shelf, which begins from the coast of Malaysia, where the sea depth does not exceed 700 feet. Irian Jaya and Aru islands lie on the Sahul Shelf, which stretches northwards from the Australian coast. Here the sea depth is similar to that of the Sunda Shelf. Located between Sunda and Sahul Shelf is the island group of Nusatenggara, Maluku and Sulawesi where the sea depth reaches 15000 feet. The land area is generally covered by thick tropical rain forests where fertile soils are continuously replenished by volcanic eruptions. The life expectancy has increased to age 64 and the population density is as follows:

Act No. 62 of 1958 governs Indonesian nationality. It defines an Indonesian national as a person who since the beginning of independence on 17th August 1945 qualifies for citizenship

**Population Density of Indonesia per Sq. Km. 1930-1980**

| | 1930 | 1961 | 1971 | 1980 |
|---|---|---|---|---|
| *Java & Madura* | 315 | 476 | 576 | 690 |
| Sumatra | 17 | 33 | 44 | 59 |
| *Kalimantan* | 4 | 8 | 10 | 12 |
| *Sulawesi* | 22 | 38 | 45 | 55 |
| Other Islands | 8 | 12 | 15 | 19 |

under existing laws. Further, a person whose mother is an Indonesian national, but whose father's nationality is unknown or whose father is stateless, shall qualify for Indonesian citizenship. Also, a person who was born in Indonesia from unknown parents, or an orphan whose parents are unknown, or a person born in Indonesia but does not inherit any nationality from his/her parents, shall qualify for Indonesian citizenship. Again a five-year-old child, who is adopted by foster parents of Indonesian nationality, shall qualify for Indonesian citizenship if the foster parents apply within a year for the same. In order to get Indonesian nationality aliens must fulfil the following conditions:

1. Have reached the age of 21,
2. Should be born in Indonesia or have lived in Indonesia continuously for 5 years uninterruptedly,
3. Have a fair command of the Indonesian language and knowledge of Indonesian history, and has never been convicted by a court for a breach of law or for any act against Indonesia,
4. Have the consent of wife/husband,
5. Are mentally and physically healthy,
6. Pay a fee of not less than Rupiah 500 and not more than Rp 10,000 which shall be decided by the court,
7. Have permanent employment,
8. Should not have another nationality nor have abandoned his/her alien nationality, which is in conformity with an

agreement on dual nationality reached between Indonesia and the foreign country.

There are about 200 languages and more than 300 dialects spoken in the whole archipelago. Some of the distinctly different languages are the Acehnese, the Batak, the Sundanese, the Javanese, the Sasak, the Tetum, the Dayak, the Minahasans, the Toraja, the Buginese, the Halmahera, the Ambonese, the Ceramese and the Papuans. The national language is Bahasa Indonesia, but local languages are spoken in different areas.

The national language of Indonesia, Bahasa Indonesia, is Malay Language as spoken in that country. Bahasa Indonesia and Bahasa Malaysia have common words, idioms and common roots, known as the Malay-Polynesian. Malay Language is spoken broadly in Indonesia, Malaysia, Brunei, Singapore and parts of the Philippines. According to historical records, Malay language was used and popularised by the Sri Vijayan rulers in the seventh century, and it remained the most important language of the archipelago ever since. Bahasa Indonesia and Bahasa Malaysia are written in an agreed common reformed spelling system, (common orthography) in both countries since 1972 and both attach importance to it as an essential part of their nationalism. It is important to have the knowledge of that language in order to get the citizenship of those countries and for aspiring civil servants and administrators. Bahasa Indonesia is written mainly in the Roman script now, which was also written in Brahmi, Pallava and Arabic scripts in the historical past.

There are more than 250 languages/dialects spoken in Indonesia of which the Acehnese, the Batak, the Sundanese, the Javanese, the Sasak, the Tetum of Timor, the Dayak, the Minahasa, the Toraja, the Buginese, the Halmahera, the Ambonese and the Ceramese are influenced by the Malay language. Their vocabulary and idioms, like Bahasa Indonesia, have indigenised a number of words from Sanskrit, Arabic, Persian, Portuguese, Dutch and English, but all of them prefer Bahasa Indonesia as their lingua franca.

Bahasa Indonesia was systematised and organised by Indonesians in the 20th century. They felt the need of a common language to evolve common nationalism. Sukarno articulated this point and there was a consensus on this issue. Hence a Youth Congress was organised in Jakarta long back in 1928. The delegates to the congress pledged to promote Malay Language as Bahasa Indonesia and nurtured it as their national language. Indonesian Nationalist Party (PNI), Sarekat Islam and Muhammadiah supported this resolution. Thereafter this language became the common medium for spreading revolutionary struggle.

The acceptability of the Indonesian language grew rapidly during the period of Japanese occupation (1942-45). The use of the Dutch language had been banned and the Japanese had ordered arresting anyone talking in the Dutch language. The textbooks for primary and secondary education, which had so far been taught in the Dutch language exclusively, were translated in Bahasa Indonesia. Hence the medium of instruction and mode of communication was replaced by Bahasa Indonesia. It is understood that the Japanese intended to replace the Dutch with the Japanese language and introduce its teachings in the schools but there was not much time to carry out such a policy.

The Japanese were given an impression that Indonesians would support their drive for "Co-prosperity" and the use of the Indonesian language in schools and official proceedings would facilitate anti-Dutch sentiments. The Japanese were propagating their war achievements and ideals for "Asia for Asians" through radio, newspapers and leaflets and they found that Bahasa Indonesia was the most important vehicle for communication in the archipelago from remotest islands to urban centers.

Japan's outstanding support to promotion of Bahasa Indonesia was witnessed with the establishment of Komisi Bahasa Indonesia (the commission for Indonesian Languages), under illustrious scholars of the era, namely Takdir Alisjahbana, Amir Hamzah and Armijn Pane. This commission performed a difficult task to provide a modern shape and systematise

Indonesian language. In order to get the feedback of their role, they published a literary magazine named Pudjangga Baru to highlight various linguistic, cultural and political issues.

As Malay language was familiar with the people along the shores of the Straits of Malacca, Sunda and Sulawesi and was understood by the people from Borneo to Moluccas, it contained many words from the area as well as from Sanskrit, Arabic, Dutch and English whose pronunciation and spelling differed from one another. The Commission for Indonesian languages simplified the spelling of many words differing from one another. They also encouraged addition and alternation of words borrowed from Javanese, Sundanese, Acehnese or Europeans.

Some basic features of Bahasa Indonesia that very often comes to our mind is that it is phonetic in character and there are very few prefixes and suffixes for verbs and nouns. It does not have gender, person, number and tense, etc., and the verb is not conditioned on the basis of conjugation, declension, tense and other complexities of grammar. It has got the indicator words which creates a system of its own through lexicon category (words).

This language is considered democratic in character, as it is without language levels of some of the languages in the neighbourhood. It can be used freely amongst all strata of the people without any difference and it is considered a common property of all Indonesian nationals. Indonesia has constitutionally declared it as the language of the state through article 36 of the 1945 constitution. President Sukarno, while elucidating the importance of Bahasa Indonesia in 1959, assured that those areas having languages of their own, such as Javanese, Sundanese, or Madurese, would also be cared for by the state. But the emphasis continued to be attached on Bahasa Indonesia.

The common language has facilitated the growth of Indonesian nationalism and proved itself as the most important facilitator of national understanding. It is through this medium that the people of Aceh, Ambon and Kupang can talk to each other and this language is increasing its vocabulary to cope with growing needs. More than 50,000 new words have been added in Today's Standard Reference Dictionary of the Bahasa compared to the Dictionary compiled by E.St. Harahap 50 years ago.

Both President Sukarno (1945-65) and President Suharto (1966-98) nurtured the developments of Bahasa Indonesia at the literary, academic and official levels. It was supported not only as a language of Indonesians but as an important bond to forge solidarity and kinship with the Malay world.

The use of the Indonesian language is gradually increasing. According to 1990 census, as recorded by the Central Bureau of Statistics, the use of Bahasa Indonesia amongst people fall into three categories. Those who use it for daily communication are 15 per cent, those who can speak but don't use it everyday are 68 per cent and those who are unable to understand it are merely 17 per cent. The efforts are made to spread the understanding of Bahasa Indonesia for every Indonesians by 2010. The liberalisation and globalisation has facilitated the spread of Indonesian language in Europe and Asia and it can be stated that Bahasa Indonesia is the symbol of national pride and spirit.

## Indonesian Muslims

The majority population in Indonesia are Muslims. They comprise 90 per cent of the population. The core of Islam rests in the Koran and the Hadith. The Koran being the collection of the words of Allah spoken by Prophet Muhammad during the years 610-622 A.D. and the Hadith collections of short narratives told by the people who knew the Prophet personally during his lifetime and which, handed down through the ages, decribe some act or saying of the Prophet which is to be taken as a guide. Taking the Koran & Hadith as given, Shariat was evolved by the Ulemas, which is also known as Muslim laws.

Clifford Geertz says: "Islam came to Indonesia from India, brought by merchants. Its mid-eastern sense for the external conditions of life having been blunted and turned inward by Indian mysticism, provided but a minimal contrast to the nelange of Hinduism, Buddhism, and animism which had held the Indonesians enthralled for almost 15 centuries".[2] Although Islam spread peacefully in the country gradually in a space of 300 years, it dominated Java in the 16th century. Indonesian Islam, cut off from its centres of orthodoxy at Mecca and Cairo, evolved a separate life style, which was not at all orthodox. Thus Buddhist mystic practices got Arabic names, Hindu Rajas changed their title to become Sultans and the common people called some of their wood spirits jinns.[3] Clifford Geertz has classified Muslims of Indonesia as the following:

(a) Santri; (b) Abangan; (c) Priyayi.

The Santri view themselves as minority representatives of the true faith in the great forest of ignorance and superstition, protectors of the divine law against the pagan crudities of traditionalised custom. It is different from the polytheistic mysticism of beliefs, which prevailed in Indonesia and was comparatively influenced by the Arab missionaries. On the other hand, Abangans believe in synthesis of the beliefs of various Koranic schools and traditional beliefs. While comparing the two, Geertz stated that Abangans are fairly indifferent to doctrine but fascinated with ritual detail, while among the Santries, the concern with doctrine almost entirely overshadows the already attenuated ritualistic aspects of Islam.[4] An Abangan knows the type of foods to be offered on ceremonial occasions, such as porridge on of the occasion of birth and pancakes at the time of death, but he will not feel upset if someone offers a different interpretation and changes the menu. Abangans are tolerant of religious beliefs and have respect for different religions. If a person does not believe in spirits or if he thinks that God lives in the sun, it is not an issue of controversy to them. But Santri considers Islamic rituals very important, especially the Namaz (the prayer). For them the knowledge of ritual detail or spiritual discipline are secondary, but the application of Islamic doctrine to life occupies primary importance. They argue that Islam is a superior ethical code for modern men, as a workable social model for modern society, and as a fertile source of values for modern culture.[5]

For the Abangan, the basic social unity to which nearly all rituals refer is the household—a man, his wife and his children. It is the household which gives the Slametan (communal feast) and it is the heads of other households who come to attend it, and then carry home part of the Slametan to the other members of their families. For a Santri, the sense of community (*Ummat*) is primary.

They believe in a society of equal believers constantly repeating the name of the Allah and the Prophet, going through the prayers and chanting the Koran. James L. Peacock says that Abangans do not seriously follow the rules of Islam, but Santri religiously adhere to these rules. The Abangan do not perform their prayer (salat) five times a day, do not fast in the month of Ramadan, have little desire to make pilgrimage to Mecca, and do not abstain from pork. The Santri are rigidly committed to all these traditions.[6]

The third group of Muslims known as Priyayis, the people of noble descent, is almost extinct in Indonesia. Priyayi indicated a man who could trace his ancestry back to the great semi-mythical kings of pre-colonial Java. The Dutch Colonial masters employed them in the administrative services and subsequently all those who came into the administrative services of the Dutch claimed to be Priyayis. They were invariably born and brought up in towns and preferred to be appointed as clerks and teachers. Geertz says that the Abangans are Indonesia's peasantry but the Priyayi are its gentry. Abangans represent the synthesis of urban imports and tribal inheritances and their tradition is a little native curing, a little tantrik magic, a little Islamic chanting, but Priyayi way of life have been different.[7] The Priyayis are very conscious of the clothes they wear, the houses they live in, the way they behave, whom they associate with, since as they associate almost exclusively with fellow Priyayis. They give utmost importance to their descent and status. They believe in peaceful assertion of their spiritual superiority, and emphasise on the inner life of refined feeling and politeness. Geertz says that Priyayi and Abangans have in many ways very similar world views, and although they share many concrete items of religious belief and practice, the ethics which can be deduced from these underlying world views and the way the items are arranged to symbolise, differ rather markedly.[8]

Indonesians believe in different kinds of spirits. They are broadly known as memedis, lelembut and tujul. Memedis of male and female are different and they usually move in the night in lonely places. They generally are frightening but harmless. Lelembut on the other hand, are regarded harmful. This spirit enters the body of a person and makes him either sick or mad. Only the native Dukun can cure this illness, otherwise the patient will die. Thirdly *tujuls* are spirit children. They neither upset nor frighten people, or make them sick or mad. Their appearances are generally regarded auspicious as their sight helps the people in becoming rich. Understanding the belief in the spirit system is very complicated as it differs from one place to another.

The Indonesians attach importance to Slametan (communal feast) everywhere. It symbolises the mystic and social unity of those participating in it. Friends, neighbours, fellow workers, relatives, local spirits, dead ancestors and goods-all get bound by virtue of their commensality into defined social groups pledged to mutual support and co-operation.[9] A Slametan can be given on any occasion one wishes to celebrate, ameliorate or sanctify birth, marriage, sorcery, death, house moving, bad dreams, harvest, name-changing, opening a factory, illness, supplication of village guardian spirit, circumcision, and starting off a political meeting. There is always special food (differing according to the intent of the *Slametan*), incense, the Islamic chant, and the extra-formal speech of the host. The occasion is given immense importance.

## Indonesian Customs

Culturally Indonesia is very rich and ethnically very diverse. Ethnicity and culture are the resultant of a multiple contending forces pulling in various directions. They include the geographical and the ethnic factors, the past events remembered by modern Indonesians with pride or shame, the cultural heritage, and the modernising forces that have given a definite direction to the course of events. As these factors have abiding influence, their broad delineation is necessary.

The word Indonesia literally means the realm of the Indian islands. At first, the term embraced all the islands between Asia and Australia, including the Philippines. The historical background of the concept of Indonesia has considerably influenced the thinking of modern Indonesia, and time and again attempts were made to unify this long chain of islands into some sort of loose political organisation. *Maphilindo* and *Asean* are the attempts in this direction. More specifically, the term Indonesia applies to the possessions of the Dutch in this part of the world, which were known as the Dutch Indies. The Indonesian archipelago is the world's largest complex of islands. It stretches from mainland Southeast Asia eastwards between Australia and Philippines. Its land area is roughly 735,000 square miles while the total land and sea area is roughly 4 million square miles. From west to east, it stretches from 95 degree to 141-degree east longitude and is spread between 6-degree north and 11 degree south latitude like a necklace of emerald strung on the equator. These geographical factors are of great relevance for a proper understanding of recent political events in this area. The Dutch frowned upon the mention of this area as Indonesia. It was in 1945 after the Proclamation of Independence that it acquired this official name.[10]

In this sprawling chain of islands, which was subject to numerous waves of migration, lived a population basically of Malay stock. With an admixture of population in different proportions on different islands, the Archipelago is the mosaic of myriads of ethnic groups, speaking innumerable dialects and having different forms of social organisations.

Distinct culture traits that were variations of a common heritage fostered a sense of exclusiveness among these various habitations. A sense of distinctiveness and local pride did tend to take at time precedence over feeling of national loyalty. And yet this cluster of islands has a personality of its own. The bewildering variety has been deftly woven into a fabric wherein colours are well blended. The coastal areas of these scattered islands had fairly good contacts due to maritime activities; a thread of common beliefs, traditions and customs that governed their primitive lives also connected isolated settlements on different islands. Beneath confusing and complex cultural layers there are some traits common to all parts of Indonesia.[11]

The indigenous culture first sprang from the animist religious practices; receptive Indonesian culture absorbed what suited it from the relentless flow of alien cultures—Hinduism, Buddhism and Islam. Christianity accommodated itself to the prevailing environment. Out of this process of evolution Indonesia developed a civilisation of its own. A vague but still powerful sense of belonging to a common heritage was the most important feature of the whole process. Western influences brought in its trail new thoughts, new values and new beliefs. But it was the Second World War, which catapulted Indonesia into the modern world. It exposed it to the challenges of the process of modernisation. The task before its leaders even today seems overwhelming and the challenges formidable. In an attempt to adopt institutions on western style to suit their needs, they look to old values, traditions, customs and warmth of the family spirit which has survived centuries of trials and tribulations.[12]

This common store of beliefs, customs and traditions still remains a strong binding force. These are generally referred to under the generic name of *Adat* (translated as Customary Law). The beliefs were inspired by the animistic, religious traditions, which believed that a spirit inhabited everything on earth. These spirits could help or hinder the efforts of mankind according to the behaviour of man towards them; if they were propitiated they would be helpful, if something was done to annoy them they would prove harmful. There were certain people well versed in the lore of magic, who knew how to propitiate the spirits and what angered them. They could also foretell the coming events through heir magical powers. This world of spirits in its turn was a part of all comprehending cosmic order that embraced in its fold the entire universe of spirits and men. There was nothing accidental in the events of the world. Each was a predictable phenomenon, which could be anticipated by a person in tune with the cosmos. Naturally, the person so versed enjoyed the highest position in the community from catastrophies. These in substance are the animistic beliefs that still exert powerful influence on the subconscious mind of the Indonesians, though Islam and contact with the modern world have eroded their hold on the conscious mind.[13]

Of still greater importance is the impact of these beliefs on the institutions that have emerged through centuries all over the Archipelago. Every village claimed a common ancestry from some spirit, which was regarded as its founder and protector. When people from outside came and settled in the village a process of stratification set in with the original inhabitants enjoying a special position. This hierarchical set-up then became an integral element of the social institutions in the village. In course of time this hierarchical setup became an integral element of the social institutions in the village council with a hereditary chief who looked after the needs and the interests of the community, assisted by a council of elders. Important decisions were taken by collective deliberations.

It was a system in which the traditional wisdom as inherited by the scion of a family with hoary traditions was supplemented by the experience and knowledge of the village elders, who were in day-to-day touch with realities. This model which exerted a powerful influence on the mind of the constitution-makers of Indonesia is shown later.[14]

This complex of socio-political organisations gave rise to certain customs and traditions that are of great significance in understanding the thinking of modern Indonesia. The pride of place in this tradition is given to Ratu Adil (literally, Goddess of Justice but also referred to as the Just Princess), a concept which gave confidence to the common man that he could always expect justice as long as he remained loyal to the Indonesian way of life. The village headman being the representative of the protecting spirit of the village was expected to render justice to all with the help of the elders who could advise him on intricate problems of law and fact. But as the final judgement came from the inspiration of the village headman himself, Ratu Adil was depended upon to do justice to the villagers.[15]

With these beliefs in a common ancestry and the protecting influence of Ratu Adil it was but natural that the villagers felt that they belonged to a common family. This feeling was enshrined in the concept of gotong-royong (mutual co-operation) or the family spirit. This is expressed in a number of ways: co-operation in fields; participation on occasions of joy and sorrow in the life of an individual by all the villagers; the sense of belonging to a common heritage. These feelings have their repercussions on the modern life of Indonesia and give it a distinctive colour. One of the consequences of this concept of gotong-royong was that a tradition grew up in which the consensus through deliberations and debates was given the pride of place as a method of arriving at a decision.

The theory of consensus is a matter of great debate in political science today, and sociological, political and economic factors are considered responsible for the insistence on consensus in increasing measure in countries throughout the world in varying degrees. The consensus as enshrined in the traditions of Indonesia had a simple source in the belief that the whole community was a family. It was only when transplanted into the deliberations of the modern assemblies that other complicating factors were injected.[16]

The concept of *bapak* (father image), which played a considerable role in the evolution of the Presidency, was also the consequence of the family spirit. Once the concept of the family is posited, the idea of the head of the family deserving special rights and privileges, and discharging special responsibilities, is a natural outcome. In Indonesian social life, the father, uncle, elder brother and cousin are the spontaneous modes of address between man and man. The nationalist movement of Indonesia derived a considerable cementing force from these sentiments. The unique position enjoyed by the President owed much to the traditional mode of social relationship. The contribution of Hinduism and Buddhism further strengthened the paternalistic approach. The institution of Rajah (king) could find an easy acceptance in Indonesia, because it was based on the idea of the king as a protector of his people. The subject looked upon the king as a dispenser of justice in conformity with the wisdom of the ages as interpreted by the leaders of the community.[17]

Then came Islam which claimed nearly 90 per cent of the population within its fold. The process of Islamisation is impregnated with seeds of assimilation and conflict. Uneven pattern of the spread of Islam affected scattered regions of Indonesia differently. It also acquired different characteristics due to historical reasons. In its long journey to Indonesia from the Middle East via Persia and India, Islam lost its proselytising fervour and vigour. In the process it acquired certain mystic characteristics which made it easier for the Hinduized regions of Indonesia to accept the faith readily. In Java and in other parts of Sumatra it was this Islam with mystic elements and not the orthodox Islam of the Middle East that held sway for a long time. But in other parts of Indonesia such as Aceh and Minangkabu region in Sumatra and Bantam in West Java, Islam in its purer form found adherents. This form was less conciliatory than the one accepted in the Hinduised regions. It was even aggressive.[18]

The process of intermingling and conflict of Islam with the prevailing culture affected different strata of Indonesian society differently. These differences continued for centuries and gave rise to three distinct cultural types, namely, *Abangan*, Santri and

Priyayi, which are still to be found in one form or the other in Indonesia.

Besides cultural values and traditions, which helped in shaping much of social norms, the historical grandeur of the powerful kingdoms, the famous religious and commercial Centres, have been influencing socio-political life of the country. Two of the kingdoms are of special importance. The first was Sri Vijaya, a maritime kingdom that flourished from the 7th to the 11th centuries. Sri Vijaya undertook the policy to break the isolation of small principalities to weave them into a larger political entity. The second was the kingdom of *Majapahit*, which was established at the end of the 13th century and flourished for almost two centuries. It covered most of the territories of Indonesia and spread in the east up to the Philippines. Gajah Madah, a great warrior and prime minister of Majapahit empire who was instrumental in the consolidation of the kingdom is remembered with pride by Indonesians as a great commander and historical figure is also remembered with his name through a University also. After the disintegration of Majapahit, the area remained under different rulers till the Dutch came and established colonial rule over the entire archipelago.

While the process of Islamisation was still going on, and while the action and interaction between Adat and Islam were creating a new culture, the Europeans started coming. First the Portuguese and then the Dutch arrived on the scene. This gave a violent jolt to the gradual cultural evolution in the area. The western powers were at first interested only in commercial activities but they developed political interests also. With the traders came soldiers and missionaries and when they found a power vacuum, they began to acquire territories, step by step and established their colonial rule.

The Portuguese came to Indonesia in 1511 in search of spices and they were followed by Spain subsequently. Besides commercial matters, these two were interested in missionary activities. They propagated Christianity at Minahasa and Moluccas

(*Maluku*) successfully, but they faced challenges from the Sultan of Aceh, Demak and Tarnate. In the meanwhile the Dutch came to Indonesia and developed colonial interests. It established a strong warship to protect merchant ships from pirate attacks and subsequently the number of warships were enlarged to protect colonial interest. After the seizure of Amboina in 1605 and Banda in 1623, the Dutch secured the monopoly over spice trade. They adopted the policy of divide and rule and hence Indonesia became dependent on the Dutch for the supply of consumer goods. The Dutch introduced new cash crops in Indonesia, which were in great demands in the European markets.

Their policy of *cultuurstelsel* changed the existing pattern of agriculture at the cost of the interest of the native population. The new policy, which was adopted in 1830, meant that the farmers had to set apart a portion of their rice fields for the cultivation of products suitable for the European market. It also meant that the portion of land set apart should amount to one fifth of the cultivated ground. The new crops, which were introduced under the system, were coffee, sugar, indigo, tea and cinnamon.[19]

Indonesia, which had been a rice producing country so far, had to switch over to production of commodities demanded by the Dutch Colonial masters and this had great repercussions on the socio-economic life of the people. In fact, this policy was opposed in Mataram and other areas in the beginning, but they were ruthlessly suppressed. Though this development was sufficient to start nationalist movement, it was delayed till the formation of Boudi Utomo in 1908, which stimulated the nationalist forces to fight unitedly against the Dutch. However, this is not the focus of inquiry here. The transformation and problems of social life that exercised influence on Indonesian society are to be evaluated for an understanding of Indonesian life.

A perusal of Indonesian social life suggests that there have been constant migrations of the people from one area to another because of geographical reasons. Since the country is a conglomeration of several islands and since they have to suffer the wrath of the ebb and flow of the tides constantly, they have to move from one place to another. Java and Sumatra had been the important areas of Subarnadwipa for centuries and there were influx of Indian settlers from first to the seventh century AD. The official handbook of Indonesia suggests that Indonesia was inhabited by sub-Mongoloid migrants from Asia, who later intermarried with the indigenous people.[20] It was natural that the people tried to migrate to different areas for better living and the government of Indonesia is conscious of it. Again it is a reality that some of the islands of Indonesia are not at all inhabited and in order to promote development at the national level, there should be manpower everywhere.

The uneven demographic factor is one of the obstacles to the development equity in Indonesia.In the country's land territory of more than 17,508 islands, only 992 islands or 7 per cent are properly inhabited. The Indonesian archipelago, stretching along the equator, has abundant natural resources, which have to be exploited to the greatest benefit of the people. The exploitation and utilisation of the natural resources will undoubtedly depend much on the human resources, remembering that man is the subject of development.

Nowadays, the potentiality of human resources is more concentrated on Java Island, which has maximum investment and growth rate. On the contrary, the development and investment in other regions outside Java are difficult to be realised due to the lack of skilled human resources and manpower.

According to the 1990 census, the total population of Indonesia was recorded at 179,321,642 and in 1994 it was about 185 million people with an average growth rate of around 1.97 per cent annually. Of the total population, 107,573,749 or 59.98 per cent lived in Java with a total area of only 6.8 per cent of the total land territory of the country. This means that the population density of Java Island is around 680.48 per sq km. Other islands such as Sumatra, Kalimantan, Sulawesi, Maluku and Irian Jaya which make up about 88.5 per cent are only inhabited by

61,583,038 people (34.34 per cent), with an estimated population density of around 36.25 per sq. km.

It is estimated that in 2020, the island of Java's population will reach approximately 143,060,615. If that happens, this island populationwise will become the biggest island city in the world. Today, the population density of Java Madura, Bali and Lombok almost reach 800 per sq. km, while that of Kalimantan with a four-fold area vaster than that of Java island, the population density is only 12 per sq. km, Maluku 20 per sq. km and even Irian Jaya with only 4 per sq. km. The moderate population density is found only on the islands of Sumatra about 59 per sq. km and Sulawesi 55 per sq. km.

At district level, the unbalanced population density is more crucial, such as Mamuju District, South Sulawesi, has a population density of 4 per sq km, *Merauke* (Irian Jaya) 2 per sq km, and *Berdu* District (*East Kalimantan*) only 1 per sq km. Whereas in Java's big cities like DKI Jakarta or the Special Territory of the Capital City Jakarta is recorded at 12,500 per sq km, and one of its sub-districts, namely Johar/Baru in the Municipality of Central Jakarta, has a population density of 51,624 per sq km.

The above-mentioned situation will clearly cause various problems–social, economic and cultural types–which are feared to damage the territorial integrity of the Republic of Indonesia. On the other hand, the agricultural areas in Java may become narrower and narrower which may lead to very low productivity of the agricultural cultivation. The agricultural sector, which absorbs almost 50 per cent of the total work force, only contributes 21 per cent of the Gross Domestic Product (GDP).

Poverty, which now hits a part of the Indonesian people, constitutes one of the resultants of the uneven distribution of the population. On the one hand, the poverty is due to their living in densely populated areas, and on the other hand, the lack of manpower in some areas have contributed to growing poverty. The government has not succeeded in exploiting the existing natural resources. The population boom in densely populated areas complicate development. Those who are keen to be prosperous, like to stay in Java. There is a brain drain from all other islands of Indonesia to Java which provides facilities in abundance.

## Transmigration

To save Java from population explosion and environmental destruction, around 60-70 million people should inhabit this island, around 37,573,749 people or around 7.5 heads of family living in Java are in excess. The best anticipated measures to tackle future challenges of the Indonesian nation are continuously being developed. Initatives are being taken to develop the islands outside Java so that people could migrate there for livelihood. Encouraging transmigration to the eastern part of the country, supporting regional development, alleviating poverty, stimulating voluntary migration, developing agro-business, agro-industry and other enterprises in transmigration areas and strengthening the institutional framework of the transmigration programme in order to improve its efficiency and effectiveness are some of the important suggestions given for a balanced development policy.

The main aim of transmigration is not the attainment of an even and balanced distribution of the population but rather the implementation of development of projects considered necessary to raise the national production. Transmigration is seen as an instrument for rural community development and the focus has been shifted from a demographic approach to a socio-economic one.

The main objective of transmigration during Repelita VI were to motivate voluntary transmigration; to provide easier access from transmigration area to market locations; to increase the transmigrates' income in an effort to generate savings for business diversification; to develop various business activities in order to achieve people's welfare living there as well as in surrounding areas. With the revocation of Government Regulation No.56 of 1958, Law No.29 of 1960 and Law No.5 of 1965, the principal legal basis of transmigration are currently Decree of the President No.1 of 1973 on Transmigrates' Place of Origin, and Decree of the President No. 2 of 1973 that designates places of destination.

The Department of Transmigration and Resettlement of Forest Squatters was responsible for all matters of transmigration. As transmigration involved various elements and fields, a co-ordinating body for the implementation of transmigration was set up at the national level with the main task of assisting the Minister of Transmigration and Resettlement of Forest Squatters in formulating short-term, medium-term and long-term integrated transmigration programs and controlling their implementation.

As stated earlier, the government protects the interests of the transmigrants and thus there has been the fusion of different cultures in the country. The common culture has synthesised the essence of Islam, Hinduism and Buddhism. They considered Shiva and Buddha as one as Mpu Tantular wrote in his book *Sutasoma.* They have evolved *Bhinneka Tunggal Ika* (Unity in Diversity) to promote solidarity amongst different religious and ethnic groups. It is observed that understanding the ethos of unity in diversity is a must for the stability and prosperity of the country. President Suharto met his downfall because he failed to maintain equilibrium between different ethnic and religious groups. There was no harmony amongst the armed forces and the Islamic groups. He could not ensure the loyalty of the Armed Forces at the end of his career and he had no alternative but to resign.

This is a fact that in order to understand Indonesian society, one must understand its mysticism. At the time of freedom struggle, the predictions of the Javanese kings and saints were popularised. The white conquerors will be followed by yellow conquerors before independence had become a reality. The white (Dutch colonial rulers) had been replaced by yellow (Japanese Colonial rulers) before independence had become reality. Similarly when Sukarno, Suharto or Wahid assumed power, there were some powerful myths behind it. Lee Khoon Choy has written in his book on Indonesia that an elite of 2000 men manipulates Indonesian politics on the basis of mysticism. Many of them are Abangans who have faith in Kobatinan (spirits which dwell in the Kris), Semar (the guardian spirit of Java), the predictions of Joyoboyo and Lara Kidul (the Queen of the Indonesian Ocean) and the Wayang (the shadow play). Based on the institutions of the aforementioned social life, there is propagation of mysticism in favour of leader or against him. It is difficult to gain a monopoly over this matter.

Thus the cultural understanding and myth of the people in different parts of the country varies from one another. The ethnic Chinese and the Melanesians, for example have different views of the social life and they have not been fully integrated in the national mainstream. The people of the Chinese descent are believed to control the economy of the country, but their loyalty to the nation are questioned. However it is also a reality that any policies directed against the Chinese will be the cause of the economic collapse of Indonesia.

To sum up, it can be stated that Indonesia is richly endowed with unique social customs and rituals. Its geographical vastness, diverse ethnic composition, tribes, cultures, traditions, dance, drama, dialects and artistic expressions are distinct. An understanding of social life on different islands in Indonesia displays diversity of culture, religion, rituals, symbols and life-style in general. Diversity is a strength as well as weakness for the nation. The immediate neighbours of Indonesia, namely Singapore, Brunei and Malaysia are prosperous and homogeneous in terms of religion and culture. They epitomise "small is beautiful", but Indonesia is vast and magnitude of its problems are heterogeneous. There is uneven development in the country and the people outside Java are unhappy with this scenario. The opposition to the government policies are articulated on the basis of religion, history, ethnicity, etc., and special anger is reserved for the ethnic Javanese.

Diversity in social life were projected as the distinctive feature of Indonesia as the leaders sought "unity in diversity", along with archipelagic principles. The political developments in the post-independence era saw that the political masters paid attention on strengthening unifying elements for national integration. National Culture, religion, symbol and literature were evaluated in the face of new challenges. Religion, an important element of nationalism, was considered an obstacle politically in the path of integration, but it assumed importance in social life through Madrasah, Pesantren and political parties.

It was the role of the Hajis to organise anti-Dutch movements. Muslims were martyred during the independence struggle, but Indonesian government did not display Islamic ethos sufficiently in the government and polity. There are a number of leaders who feel that resurgence of Islam and assertion at the political level would assure the prosperity of the nation. Darul Islam, Muhammadiyah, Sarekat Islam, etc. have established political role of Islam. It is due to their preachings that militant groups such as *Jemaah Islamiyah* and Islamic Defender's Forum have emerged. They are armed with weapons and talks about Jehad. Their activities have provoked non-Muslims to react. Similar is the experience in Kashmir and some other parts of the world.

Although the Islamic faith is the predominant religion, Indonesian society is not at all homogeneous despite the existence of common geographical problems, common history (*Srivijaya* and *Majapahit*s), common struggle against colonial rule, common cultural ethos and common concern for development. The substantial success is visible in the promotion of Bahasa Indonesia which is the national language as well as lingua franca of the entire nation. Bahasa Indonesia connects the people of Indonesia from one region to another and it has assumed importance for Indonesian society and politics. But language alone cannot stop the tendency for fragmentation. Economic development and good governance are needed to evolve favourable socio-economic environment.

## References

1. Indonesia (1987) An Official Handbook, p.19
2. Clifford Geertz, the Religion of Java, New York, 1969, pp 124-25.
3. *Ibid.*, p.125.
4. *Ibid.*, p.127.
5. *Ibid.*
6. *Ibid.*
7. *Geertz*, N.5, p.229.
8. *Ibid.* p.235
9. *Ibid.*
10. Satyavati S. Jhaveri, Presidency in Indonesia, Bombay 1975, p.11.
11. *Ibid.*, p.12
12. *Ibid.*, p.12
13. *Ibid.*, p.13
14. *Ibid.*, p.14
15. *Ibid.*
16. *Ibid.*
17. *Ibid.*, p.15.
18. *Ibid.*, Also see for better perspective, R.S. Kipp & S. Rodgers Indonesian Religion in Transitions, Tucson, 1987.
19. D.G.E.Hall, A History of Southeast Asia, London, 1968, p.547.
20. Indonesia, 1997, An Official Handbook, p.19.

# 3

# Religion in Indonesia

Indonesia is a vast country of multi-religious background. Religion indeed plays an important and decisive role in the socio-political life of the country. Though Indonesia has not declared secularism as the guiding principle of the state constitutionally, it has endeavoured to pursue a secular path. The Panchasila as followed by Sukarno (1945-65) and Suharto (1966-98) believes in secular policies. However, the major political parties and elite groups play religious cards to promote their political interests. It is an important instrument to be wielded in the struggle for power. The militant groups are also advocating their case on the basis of religion. The turmoil in Aceh, Irian Jaya, Ambon and Nusa Tenggara can be explained in religious terms and this factor is important to analyse contemporary politics in Indonesia.

In fact, religion always played an important role in Indonesian politics. It is considered an integral part of their nationalism. The religious centres (Pesantren, Mosques, Temples and Church) had been extensively used for political purposes during the freedom struggle. As the mosque, temple and church are holy places for social congregation and education, they play significant role in mobilisation of national awakening and renaissance. Again the cultural programmes, namely, music, dance, drama, *wayang* (shadow plays) and puppet shows selected religious themes to arouse patriotism. The Pesantren and missionary schools played significant role in the socialisation of the people, and in the garb of religion, they succeeded in arousing nationalist feelings.

When Indonesia became independent in 1945, various religious groups had their own agenda and it was difficult to synthesise them into a nationalist framework. Though Sukarno was charismatic, he evaded a definite answer to this complex issue. Islamic groups were active for Islamisation at the time of framing of the constitution and were demanding full recognition of Islam as a state religion. Naturally this demand was opposed by others including those advocating archipelagic concept. The Constituent Assembly (*Badan Penjelidik Kemerdekaan Indonesia, BPKI*) discussed the issue and came out with a compromise formula. Thus a document was signed, known as Djakarta Charter on 22 June 1945. Accordingly it was decided that the fundamental laws of the Indonesian state shall be based upon "Belief in God, with the obligation of practising the laws of Islam for the adherents of that religion in accordance with the principles of just and civilised humanity".[1] Though the Islamic groups were not fully satisfied with the compromise, the main concern of the leaders then was declaration of independence. The Dutch colonial masters who wanted to regain control of Indonesia was the major challenge to cope with. The nationalist leaders argued that religious demands can be accommodated after the departure of the external invaders, and this proved a decisive factor in striking the compromise.

When the Dutch colonial masters finally left in 1949, Sukarno started fighting for sovereign rights over West Irian. The public opinion was diverted on discussing several issues like socialism, land reforms, Ganjang Malaysia and other factors. He did not allow religious groups to assert in political matters. His successor, General Suharto imposed military rule and clamped restrictions on political parties. He, however took the help of religious groups whenever it suited him. He undertook a pilgrimage to Mecca and thereafter he preferred to be called a *Haji*. His authoritarian rule was long (1966-1998) but he had to resign when Indonesia came into the grip of financial crisis. The departure of Suharto from Presidency paved the path for democratic system in Indonesia. Hence political parties and pressure groups have emerged and under the situation religion indeed is a dominant factor in the struggle for power. There is a greater challenge for and against Islamisation and there is an urgent need for working out a middle path on the model of Jakarta Charter once again. However, there are some political parties and militant groups who are abhorrent of the middle path and argues in favour of Islamisation at the state level.

In order to understand the role of religion in Indonesian society, we should try to understand population distribution at the national level. The Muslims are in majority, but minorities comprise the dominant population in certain areas. For instance, Hindus are in majority in Bali and Protestants are dominant population in Batak (North Sumatra). Again Catholics are in majority at East Nusa Tenggara and Irian Jaya. Culturally Indonesia is heterogeneous. Though the majority in Aceh are also Muslims, their life-style and customs differ with their counterparts in Java. The plurality and heterogeneity as displayed in Indonesia is a unique phenomenon, compared to their counterparts in West Asia. Indonesia has been very tolerant and sensitive to the existence of other religious groups and as a result, Christianity, Hinduism and Buddhism continue to exist. The break-up of the population on the basis of religion is the following:

| | |
|---|---|
| Muslims | 87.2 per cent |
| Protestants | 6 per cent |
| Catholics | 3.5 per cent |
| Hindus | 2 per cent |
| Buddhists | 1 per cent |

Indonesia officially recognise the existence of five religions namely Islam, Protestantism, Catholicism, Hinduism and Buddhism. The government is committed to promote harmonious nature of religious life and interaction. It has not declared any state religion at the state level and all religions are regarded equal in the eyes of the law. The government has been offering generous grants for the maintenance of religious places without any discrimination and hence it believes in the principles of secularism. The declared goal of the 1945 constitution also mentions "belief in the one God Almighty", which has been interpreted in different ways. For Muslims it is Allah Almighty, but this understanding is not binding upon other religious groups. They have freedom to worship their own Gods and pursue their own customs and traditions. Article 29 of the 1945 constitution explains that the state is based on the belief in one God Almighty and the state does not separate itself from religious life and values of its citizens, though it does not declare a state religion.[2] However the problem arises from the fact that Java, one of the 17508 islands of Indonesia, constitute 65 per cent of the population. Javanese leaders and intellectuals do believe that they are people of wisdom and self-control. Like Brahmins in India, their interpretations of religious and cultural values were acceptable to others but now the situation is in transition. The traditional and cultural values of Javanese teach them to live in harmony with all human beings regardless of their faith and convictions,[3] but when the question of sharing power with others arise, their preferences apparently are for the Javanese. Thus the people of other islands project them as parochial and it creates potentials for conflict. Indonesia being so large and heterogeneous, it is not easy to prevent divergence of viewpoints and perspectives. President Sukarno, President Suharto and President Abdurrahman Wahid hails from Java, and it is difficult for the leaders of other islands to lead the nation. At the same time, it is necessary for a national leader to testify their dedication towards Islamic culture and values, without which their credentials to lead the nation have no meaning.

The guidelines of State Policy of 1945 constitution mentions the objective of maintaining religious harmony in an effort to strengthen the unity and oneness of the Indonesian people. It has offered opportunities to religious groups to practice their faith, and has been supporting the maintenance and activities of 550,676 mosques, 29,105 Protestant churches, 68,974 Hindu temples, 12,896 Catholic churches and 3,160 Buddhist *Viharas*.[4]

Indonesian history has proved that it opened its doors at different stages to Hinduism, Buddhism, Christianity and Islam to spread its influence and they became important religions of the country.

Hinduism went to Indonesia thousands of years ago. There are references about Javadwipa in the great epic, in Kishkindha Kand of Valmiki Ramayana. Though we have very little information about the history before the Christian era, but there are evidences to believe that Hinduism was rampant as the archaeological findings suggest. In 144 A.D. when Chinese traveller, Fa Hsien was caught in a storm and landed inadvertently at Javadwipa, he noted that the northern part of the island was then ruled by a Hindu King, named Kudungga. On the other hand, Kutai, on the island of Borneo, was successively ruled by Hindu Kings, namely *Devawarman, Aswawarman and Mulawarman.*

George Coedes has written that Sanjaya dynasty of *Mataram* (Central Java) in the beginning of the Christian era were Hindus. They worshipped Lord Shiva and built many Shiva temples. Whenever the kings conquered a new territory, they built new Chandi temples. Shailendras, who succeeded in defeating the Sanjayas, established Srivijayan empire and had embraced Buddhism. They are believed to be extremely sensitive to preserving Hindu customs and traditions, and while building Buddhist temples, they reserved some places for Hindu Gods. The Chinese annals mentioned the existence of Kanto Lim *(Srivijaya)* in South Sumatra, presently in Palembang. It was ruled by Gautam Subhadra, Pirawarman and Vinaywarman respectively, who had excellent relations with Han rulers in China. The Chinese traveller I Tsing, who visited Srivijaya in 671 A D, on his way to India, noted that Srivijaya was a famous centre of Buddhist learning. The well known scholars of the era adoring the courts of the *Srivijayan* rulers were *Sakyakirti, Dharmapala* and *Vajabudhi.*

Shailendras gradually shifted their capital to central Java. During their rule (750-850 A D), the famous Buddhist temple of Borobudur was built. Borobudur temple is a wonderful monument and considered important structure of the world heritage. It is a huge stupa. The walls of the galleries on both sides are adorned with bas-relief sculptures illustrating Mahayanist cults. There are 400 images of Lord Buddha and series of reliefs depicting the affects of good and evil deeds in daily life producing Karma.[5] Shailendras also built the temples of Mendut, Kalasan and Pawan, which is presently located in the city of Yogyakarta. On the other hand, one Shiva temple was built in 675 AD on the Dieng mountain range (Mataram) and Prambanan temple dedicated to Lord Shiva was built by King Daksha in 900 A D.[6]

During 911-1007 AD, the powerful kingdom of Singasari emerged in East Java under king Dharmawangsa. He codified laws and translated *Mahabharata* into Javanese. He also ordered the translation of Hindu holy book, Bhagwat Gita. His contemporary, king Airlangga of Bali had strong faith in Hinduism. Before his death in 971 AD, he divided his kingdom into two parts, namely Janggla and Kediri, to be ruled by his two sons. King Jayabaya of Kediri (1135-1157) had great interests in astrology, who made a prophecy that his country is on the threshold of downfall and it would be ruled by a white race followed by a yellow race, which proved correct. Indonesia came under the Dutch colonial rule (white) followed by the Japanese (yellow) before regaining its independence.

Majapahit period (1293-1520) is however regarded epoch making in the history of Indonesia. King Vijaya (Kartarajasa) and Hayam Wuruk of this period were great warriors and they had expanded the boundaries of the country up to *Champa* (Vietnam) and the Philippines. King Wuruk's premier, Gajah Mada, who is the hero of Indonesian folk tales till today, had united the island areas of Southeast Asia in the name of Dwipatara. *Majapahit* rulers gave patronage to its intellectuals and promoted their literary contributions. *Prapancha* (1335-1380) wrote *Negara Kertagama*, in which economic and diplomatic policies of the government were discussed. Other writings were *Pararaton, Arjuna Wiwah*, *Ramayana*, ***Saras** Muschaya* in *Kawi* (old Javanese Language).

Majapahit rulers believed in Buddhism but Hindu customs and traditions were not ignored. At the same time, they observed the customs of animism also. They were open hearted in religious matters and allowed interaction with Islamic Saints, which influenced Indonesian society in due course. They accepted Islam, but continued to pursue customs of Hinduism, animism and Buddhism along with their new religion.

Majapahit Kingdom was prosperous and therefore traders were coming from different areas. The Muslim merchants from Gujarat and Persia and later Sufi Saints started propagating Islam and became successful in converting the king of Demak to Islam. Thereafter the kings of Sirebon, Banten and Gresik accepted Islam. They collectively fought against Majapahit rulers and assured the downfall of the Kingdom. Thus Islamic movement became very strong and was embraced by the people of the archipelago as their common religion. When Islamic rulers were consolidating their position, European colonial masters came to the area. The Portuguese who came to the area in 1511 in connection with the spice trade, established their foothold in the area after the conquest of Malacca. They were interested not only in business and trade, but also in converting the people to accept Christianity. They succeeded in their mission in some areas of the Indonesian archipelago.

Thus we find that the Indonesians were accommodative and magnanimous while welcoming the religious missionaries. They displayed tolerance towards religious shrines even after massive conversion from one religion to another. Various Hindu temples are very well preserved till today. Buddhist Stupa of Borobudur is regarded as an important symbol of their national heritage. There is no story of destruction as in India of Somnath temple, Nalanda, Kashi and Mathura. There has been no scandal on the pattern of Babri Masjid. Hindu, Buddhist and Islamic shrines are respected and they are regarded common heritage of Indonesian people. It is a reality that Indonesian historians project their history from the beginning of the Christian era till the 16th century as Hindu Indonesian period. They emphasise that their culture and civilisation have emanated through syncretisation of Hindu, Buddhist and indigenous cultural elements. They also attach credit to India for their traditional system of government, ancestry system, organisation of military, literature, music, dance, architecture, religious practices and rituals. The epics of Mahabharata and Ramayana are popular through wayang (shadow play) in all parts of Indonesia. The most important matter to be noted is that Indonesians do not hesitate in speaking that Hindu influence is deep-rooted. The contrast is the case of Afghanistan and Pakistan, which had been the main centre of Hindu civilisation, in the beginning of the Christian era but they dislike to speak about their Hindu periods in the past.

Indonesian and the Dutch historians have been saying that Islam came to Indonesia through India. While mentioning this, noted Dutch scholar Clifford Geertz in his famous book, The Religion of Java says, "Islam came to Indonesia from India, brought by merchants. Its Mid-Eastern sense for the external conditions of life having been blunted and turned inward by Indian mysticism, provided but a minimal contrast to the melange of Hinduism, Buddhism and animism which had held the Indonesian enthralled for almost 15 centuries. Although it spread peacefully for the most part through almost all of Indonesia in a space of three hundred years and completely dominated Java by the end of the 16th century, Indonesian Islam, cut off from its centres of orthodoxy at Mecca and Cairo, vegetated, another meandering tropical growth on an already overcrowded religious landscape. Buddhist mystic practices got Arabic names, Hindu Rajas suffered a change of title to become Muslim Sultans, and the common people called some of their wood spirits Jinns; but little else changed".[7]

Bali is one of the important islands where Hinduism continues to remain the dominant religion. Though the population is around 30 lakhs only, culturally it is rich. Their spiritual roots are strong and they remain artistic in all walks of life. Their colourful cremation pyres are incredible and rituals and customs are unique.

Bali has been the citadel of Hindu religion and culture. When Java and Sumatra became Islamic in the 16th Century, there was a large exodus of Hindu aristocracy, priests, artists and artisans from all over the country to Bali and it became a major centre of Hindu religion, art and culture. Though Bali remained autonomous for a long time, subsequently the Dutch colonial masters came and it became a Dutch colony. But its Hindu religion and culture continued to flourish. When on 17th August 1945 Indonesia became independent, Bali became one of its important provinces. The new government tried to promote best traditions, customs and folk tales of Hindus and provided patronage to Hindu temples and religious trusts.

The Hinduism in Bali, however is different from Hinduism in India in certain matters. They do have a caste system but there are no untouchables. In fact, the only thing that reflects the hierarchical system is the language which have three (3) tiers, namely low, middle and high Balinese. Majority speaks low Balinese. Middle Balinese is rarely spoken which is used for talking to strangers. Again high Balinese is used while talking to the highest class, the Brahmins (Pendanda) which have lot of words from *Kawi*, the ancient Javanese language.

Balinese worship the Hindu Trinity Brahma, Shiva and Vishnu. Other Indian Gods like Ganesh are also worshipped, besides many Gods and spirits that are uniquely Balinese. They strongly believe in magic powers and spirits and they are exponents of *Tantra Vidya* (the science of invoking spirits). They believe that good spirits dwell in the mountains and bad spirits in the ocean. Most villages in Bali have atleast three main temples namely *Purapuseh* facing the mountains dedicated to village founders; second, *Pura Desa* normally found in the centre, dedicated to the welfare of the village and third, *Pura Dalem* facing the Sea, is dedicated to the spirits. The tales of *Ramayana* and *Mahabharata* and other stories of Hinduism are the inspiring force in dance and drama of Balinese society.[8]

## Muslim Community

Indonesian Muslims are by and large syncretists and they have tried to nurture their indigenous culture and civilisation. Though the majority believes in Islamic faith, they are not fanatics. They have allowed the growth of different faiths and religion. The life style of Indonesian Muslims differ from one another. Java, which inhabits the majority of the population, has three types of Muslims. Clifford Geertz has identified them as the following:

(i) Abangan
(ii) Santri, and
(iii) Priyayi (Prijaji)

Abangan is avowedly tolerant and most syncretic and their Islam reflect the essence of traditional beliefs, mysticism, Hinduism and Buddhism. Abangan does not believe in Islamic orthodoxy. They have liberal views regarding their Islam whereby they treat Ramayana, Mahabharata, Bhagwat Gita, Tripitaka and Bible as part of their culture. The majority of Indonesian Muslims are Abangans. Santri, on the other hand, attach much more importance to Islamic laws in their daily life and strive for Islamic purity. They look towards Islam for social and moral interpretations and Islam is given central place in their perspective. Though their numbers are small compared to Abangans, their role in politics are influential.

Lastly, the *Priyayi* population is almost extinct. In fact, they were Java's aristocratic elites, clustered around courts of various kingdoms and socially and financially influential. They were refined and sophisticated and their views of Islam were liberal. They were preferred in the administrative system of various *Sultenate*s and thereafter by the colonial government. Their numbers rapidly decreased after the end of the colonial rule, especially when Sukarno started socialistic drives. The Muslim

Community of Indonesia tend to reflect the best customs and traditions of the ethnic Malays but there has been an influx of philosophical and ideological thinking and debates for a change which may ultimately decide the destiny of the nation.

The core of Islamic faith rests in the *Koran* and the *Hadith*—the *Koran* being a collection of words of Allah spoken by Prophet Muhammad and the *Hadith* is a collection of short narratives told by the people who knew the Prophet personally during his lifetime. Based on *Koran* and *Hadith* is *Shariat*, the Muslim laws to be obeyed by its adherents.

*Koran* is universally accepted but *Hadith* runs into thousands of sayings. Because it is based on hearsay, its authencity deserves to be scrutinised. Again based on *Koran* and *Hadith* are *Shariat* laws. A section of the people attach religious sanctity to *Shariat* but *Abangan* does not do so. Therefore, there is a difference of opinion on adopting Islamic laws. This is one of the important issues in the differences between the separatists in Aceh and the central government. It is in this connection that Anders Uhlin in his book, 'Indonesia and the Third Wave of Democratisation' stated: "Many Indonesian Muslims, especially in Java, are not orthodox. They are syncretists who believe not only in Allah and the *Koran*, but also in various kinds of spirits. They adhere to pre-Islamic ceremonies and rituals, and stress the inner content instead of the formal aspects of the religion".[9]

The government has been very sensitive to religious matters. In line with the guidelines of state policy and in order to promote social harmony and balance, the government has evolved several measures. The official Handbook of Indonesia (1997) has pointed out seven areas in the religious sector where the government is paying special attention, which are as follows:

(i) Religious information and guidance,
(ii) Infrastructure for religious pursuits,
(iii) *Haj* Pilgrimage,
(iv) Promotion of Religious education in Primary and Secondary Schools,
(v) Maintenance of Religious institutions,

(vi) Religious Research and Development, and

(vii)Promotion of Women's role in social affairs.

The religious information and guidance were being provided to 930 groups, consisting of 640 Muslim, 90 Protestant, 120 Catholic, 40 Hindu and 40 Buddhist groups in 1995-96. This is to promote organisational level interaction amongst different religious groups. The government promotes publication and dissemination of religious information and 16 thousand packages of Islamic teachings are circulated. For religious tolerance, meetings amongst religious leaders and their interaction with the government leaders are organised. Again *Koran* recital competition (*Musabaqah Tilawatil Quran*) is regularly organised. On the other hand, the church chorus activities (*Pesparawi*) for the Protestant and Catholics, *Lontar* and *Bhagwat Gita* reading contest for the Hindus and *Dharmpad* reading for the Buddhists are regularly organised. The government also aids the construction of marriage halls and marital advisory council to offer services to the various communities to promote social welfare.

The government also supports assistance to renovate and construct the places of worship, and rehabilitate them. The total number of places of worship supported in 1995-96 were 594.4 thousand mosques, 30.8 thousand Protestant churches, 13.6 thousand Catholic Churches, 23.7 thousand temples, 3.9 thousand Buddhist *Viharas*. As far as rehabilitation of religious places are concerned, the government assisted 2.2 thousand mosques, 179 Protestant Churches, 162 Catholic Churches, 139 temples and 52 *Viharas*. The government offers services to *Haj* Pilgrims by assisting them to adopt appropriate procedures, preparation and departure, to go to Saudi Arabia and return back. It has established *Haj* dormitories at five locations namely in the special territory of *Jagyakarta*, *Jambi, Palang Karya, Sumarinda* and *Jayapura*. The government co-ordinates with various Muslim organisations to facilitate *Haj* Pilgrims in all the provinces.

The government of Indonesia promotes religious education at primary and secondary schools. This programme includes upgrading the courses for religious understanding, publication of religious text books, guide books and the construction of new class rooms. So far as the secondary schooling is concerned, religious education for *Madarsah Aliyah* (Islamic Senior High School) has been supported. In 1995-96 the number of *Madarsah Aaliyah* (MA) were 39 thousands consisting of 457 state run and 26 thousand private run schools. The government has also constructed thousands of school buildings, language laboratories and libraries and provides text books to promote religious knowledge and understanding.

Programme of religious research and development is aimed at supporting the formulation of policy, planning as well as development of religious life, while the programme of law counselling is aimed at imparting knowledge of Western View of jurisprudence and Islamic laws in different parts of the world. This is to make the law conscious community in the religious fields to be fair and impartial. This is directed towards the enhancement of the concept of rule of law in the judicial system so that they can support the development of national law and national perspective.

Finally, women's role in social affairs are promoted so that they can play leadership role. They are given counselling to participate in family welfare programmes and encouraged to take part in debates. This has proved extremely useful in implementation of family planning programmes. It is quite interesting to know that unlike some Islamic countries, Indonesia does not make any distinction between the rights of men and women. Both are given equal rights in education, law, health, political participation and employment.[10] The efforts have been made to offer equitable opportunities to women to take part in national development and modernisation.

They have access to important positions in the cabinet, armed forces and the civil service. The government has promoted the formation of women's organisations in various walks of life and thus Indonesian Women's Organisation (KOWANI) has been powerful in which 64 women's organisations are affiliated. These organisations are either professional or religious groups of women. KOWANI maintains co-operation not only with government agencies, but also with ASEAN Confederation of Women's Organisations (ACWO) and the International Council for Women (ICW).

## Islamic Resurgence

All these policies suggest that the government has endeavoured to use religion for nation building and modernisation and is conscious of pursuing and maintaining 'Unity in diversity". However, the existing realities show disturbing trends. There are some Islamic groups advocating religious revivalism. They want to prove themselves as much religious in temperament and behaviour as their counterparts in Iran or Saudi Arabia. They are keen to show that they are equal to their co-religionists in the Muslim heartland in terms of applying Islamic ethos. They are reflecting their opinion to implement *Shariat* laws and enforce the routine of daily prayer, circumcision rites, *Ramazan* fast and pilgrimage on state level. *Koranic* exigencies, dogmas, jurisprudence and eschatology are highlighted for nation building. They also advocate *Jehad* for the perceived enemy in the society. It is thus pertinent to know as to why such a phenomenon is occurring in a society, which had been tolerant and human for centuries.

The quest for Islamic resurgence in Indonesia is a new phenomenon. It has been caused due to several reasons. First and most important is the external factor, particularly the Arab World. The Islamic world and Muslim Ummah faced peculiar challenges in the beginning of 1970s. The Islamic revolution in Iran under Ayatollah Khomeini, the Soviet invasion on Afghanistan, the shooting incident at Masjidil Haram (Saudi Arabia) and Arab-Israel war drove the Muslim world to forge greater solidarity with one another at the global level. The countries in West Asia took advantage of its conflict with Israel and raised the price of oil and natural gas exorbitantly. This enriched them to exercise power at the international level. They started aiding and abetting Islam at the global level. Libya, Saudi Arabia and Iran started taking interests in rejuvenating Islam internally and externally and it was natural for them to pay attention to Indonesia, the largest country of the Muslim World. As a result, some Islamic groups in Indonesia started advocating Islam as an all encompassing way of life (al-din), superior to other religions. They began to display assertion in espousing Islamic fundamentalist values, ideals and solutions, and emphasised the role of the organisation to make them more organised and effective at the state level.[11]

There is a trend towards Islamic resurgence at the Southeast Asian level also. The religious groups through their theological and intellectual publications, namely, Pesantren in Indonesia, Risalah in Malaysia, Al Rabitah in Thailand and Sedar in Singapore, have highlighted the case of Islamic resurgence, and the impact of their writings are deep-rooted amongst a section of Muslim elites. They aspire the formation of a state that would resort to the *Koran* and *Sunnah* as the sources of law and place the *Alim-Ulama* at the apex of the state leadership. Thailand has a sizeable Muslim population in Patani areas and the Philippines have in Sulu and Mindanao. Being dominant in certain areas, they are demanding autonomy or independence to maintain their Islamic identity. There have been serious violences in those areas led by Muslim fanatics in the past few decades.

Again *Brunei Darussalam* and Malaysia which have the majority of Muslims and which have declared Islam as the state religion, also witness the movement for Islamic resurgence. Although Islamic laws are applied in regulating family matters such as marriage, divorce and inheritance, fundamentalists believe that the government is not doing much for Islam and the Muslims.They want reflection of *Koran* and *Sunnah* at the apex of state leadership. Their influence are increasing and as a result more and more Muslims are attending religious classes. The Muslim students are easily distinguishable from others by their dress and address. Their popular dresses are *Songkok, Julbab,*

*Sarban, Telekong*—Mini and *Purdah* (*Burka*) and their style of addressing (greeting) is *Assaamulaikum.*

The fundamentalist ideas are getting support through Muslim missionary activities, called *Dakwah*, which is generously supported by the oil-rich West Asian countries. *Dakwah* missionaries have succeeded in influencing urban population in Malaysia and inculcated Islamic consciousness on a scale never witnessed in the past. The Sultenate of Brunei is very sensitive to *Dakwah* activities, and has been compelled to prove that it protects Islamic interests. It has been making bigger financial allocation to build Mosques and *Madrasas*. It has been generously aiding the upgradation of Islamic lessons and text books in the school curriculum. However, these measures are not sufficient to dilute the appeal of the Dakwah.

Malaysia, with a contiguous border with Indonesia, is facing the upsurge of fundamentalist ideas. The *Dakwah* activities led by *Abim, Darul Arqam, Jamaat Tabligh* and *Perkim* are critical of the government policies. Their appeal under the patronage of PAS (Islamic Party of Malaysia) and ABIM (Malaysian Islamic Youth Movement) have increased. The government is concerned about it and Prime Minister, Mahathir Mohamad has been taking several measures to cope with the situation. He has been announcing some policies and perspectives supporting greater Islamisation. Yet his credentials as an Islamic leader is questioned. His administration has established Islamic banks, Islamic insurance, Islamic Economic Foundation, Special Islamic Enforcement Group, International Islamic University, Islamic Medical Centre, Puset Islam (the nerve centre of Islamic Bureaucracy) and the government has made official declaration of "Islamisation of the government machinery".[12] These steps are apparently to refute the allegation that *Mahathir* government is not doing much for Islam and the Muslims. It is trying to convince its Muslim population that his administration would always safeguard Muslim interests and also that it is committed to promote Islam at the national and international levels.[13]

Malaysia is indeed facing problems in its Islamisation process. It is multi-ethnic society, where ethnic Chinese have a sizeable population. Though ethnic Malay Muslims dominate politically and their dominant rights are reserved constitutionally, it is not easy for them to find out a common identity acceptable to all the three important ethnic groups, *i.e.* Malays, Chinese and the Indians. All of them may be patriots but when the question comes to foster and promote Islam as the foundation of national culture and identity, there is no unanimity. The country since its independence, has nurtured democratic institutions, secular norms, pluralism and humanitarian ethos and it is not easy to impose Islam on others arbitrarily. The Muslims might be more assertive, but that may prove counter productive in due course. A number of Islamic fanatics may be organised and armed with sophisticated weapons in some areas, but their actions have no support of law.

Though dominated by Muslims, there are clear differences in attitudes and opinions of Islamic leaders and intellectuals on the question of Islam in politics and Islamic fundamentalism. There are differences in details governing the principles of faith on Islamic concepts such as *Aldin, Tawheed* and *Aqeedah* as well as the modus operandi of the Islamic state in the modern environment. However the quest for unification and globalisation of Islamic world and the endeavour to link "peripheral" Muslims with their counterparts in the Muslim "heartland" in letter and spirits, are motivating factors for the fundamentalists to work for Islamic assertion in Southeast Asia.

The issue of religion in Indonesia is more or less similar on the pattern of Malaysia. There is a quest for assertion of religious values and symbols and *Harakah* groups are active. They have been arguing for the establishment of *Negara* Islam Indonesia and replacement of Panchasila with Islam as the foundation of state philosophy. The attempts towards revitalisation of the Islamic spirits have been accentuated through some organisations, namely Darul Islam and Ikhwanul Muslimin. These organisations have sought to transform their *modus operandi* from ordinary organisational activities into that of an Islamic movement. They draw their inspiration from the life and practices of the Prophet Mohammed, the *Koranic* Generation of the *Sahbahs* (Prophet's close companions) as well as from the ideas and programmes of more recent *Harakah* (cause oriented) movements like *Jamate* Islam*i*. They have given attention to their planning, methodology, operations and special training to display their militancy. They are committed to sacrifice their lives to attain their objectives. They attach importance to education (*Tarbiyah* and *Usrrah*) under the supervision of alimulama (pious Islamic scholars), with a message that goes beyond rituals to generate special identity. The leaders of Islamic movements are mostly graduates of secular Western Universities and they tend to operate more from the cities than from rural areas.[14]

Thus Indonesia has been facing challenges through religious groups but its beginning can be traced ever since its independence. Masjumi Party (Majlis Sura Muslim Indonesia) influenced by the teachings of Mohammed Abduh of Cairo University, which had mobilised support of the Muslims in Sumatra, South Sulawesi and West Java, was highly critical of Marxist oriented socialism of Sukarno. It had posed serious problems to Sukarno administration particularly when guided democracy was declared. Masjumi leaders argued that a renewed Islam was capable of providing a religious and philosophical base for rapid social and economic development. It believed in challenging Panchasila based Indonesia to one based on Islam. Mohammed Natsir, a Masjum*i* leader pleaded that since Islam was the religion and philosophy of most Indonesians, the Islamic majority need not accept a nation based on secular Panchasila, because secularism is an alien concept. This Party was advocating the inclusion of *Shariat* laws in the constitution and their activities created serious problems for Sukarno administration. Hence his government moved to ban this organisation. Though this party was officially banned, its appeal continued to exist.

In fact, the role of religious groups and missionaries cannot be overlooked in the context of Indonesia because of their constructive role in the freedom struggle. It was *Hajis* (visiting Mecca on pilgrimage) who worked for anti-colonial struggle. Whenever they returned after their pilgrimage, they felt the need of independence, Islamic political order, purification and even outright assertion against the colonial masters. They began to express their critical views about the political system. They began to evaluate and review the role of their social and religious institutions which helped the colonial rulers to perpetuate their rule. It was common for Hajis and their circle of followers to express critical views about *Adat*, (customs and traditions of Islam) which were making them subservient to the colonial rulers. One of them, named Haji Muhammad Rifangi who led Buduah movement among the rural population of Pekalongan and Kediri advocated religious reforms. He tried to mobilise public opinion to boycott official rituals in the *Kalisalak* mosque. The Dutch colonial government was annoyed so much so that *Rifangi* was exiled to *Moluccas*.

Another Haji who became a national figure was Haji Abdul Karim of Banten. He established a Pesantren School in Banten and tried to evolve Islamic political thinking. He travelled throughout Banten holding purification rights, Ziki and holy processions. He was regarded very devout possessing divine powers. He was one of the first, who had predicted inevitability of *Jehad* (war for the survival of Islam, the arrival of Mahdi and subsequently the ushering of a new era.[15]

Hajis had always played significant role in the nationalist upsurge. Whether it was Boedi Oetomo or Sarekat Islam, they were born with the support and insight of the Hajis. Boedi Oetomo established by Indonesian intellectuals in 1908 for educational purposes, started working for political consciousness. Subsequently Sarekat Islam was born in 1912 under the leadership of Haji Samanhudi. Though the apparent objective of *Sarekat* Islam was to strengthen business relations with the Dutch empire, it turned out to be a political party under the leadership of H.O.S. Tjokroaminoto, *Haji* Agoes Salim and others. *Hajis* had played significant role in the establishment of Muhammadiah also in the same year under the leadership of K.H. Ahmad Dahlan in Jogyakarta. Again Partai Indonesia was formed by Setiabudi, Tijito Mangunnkusumo and K.I. Hajar Dewantoro in the same year.

The religious groups in Aceh made great contributions for violent revolution against the colonial masters. The Pesantren and the *Ulemas* mobilised training for freedom fighters.[16] One of the famous leaders of Aceh was Tengku Cik Tiro, who contributed new insights in the nationalist upsurge. He was educated and trained in Pesantren but was extremely critical of the Dutch colonial system. He, with the support of some *Ulemas*, had established links with reformist Muslims and other anti-colonial forces. The nationalists in Aceh had taken up arms to fight battles against the Dutch colonial forces. The leaders like Tiro propagated guerrilla warfare and preferred jungles and mountains to confront the enemy. The leaders in Aceh was successful in indoctrinating the nationalist forces with the help of religion.

They preached that the blessings of the Allah are unlimited for those who serve for community and fight for the Muslim nation. All those who are ready to serve and sacrifice, are dear to the Allah, who gives name, fame and wealth to dear and devouts. He blesses paradise full of light to martyrs. Their appeals had long-term implications. The Dutch colonial forces were unable to control them effectively and independence did not mean much for them because the new rulers also could not fulfil their dreams of an Islamic state.

In short, it can be stated that the interplay of religion with society is key to understanding Indonesian politics. Japanese invaders knew this and nurtured the activities of Islamic institutions to neutralise the Dutch. Islamic leaders were anti-Dutch in their activities and temperament and therefore they supported the Japanese as friends to throw out the Dutch colonial rulers. Sukarno, the father of the nation, however was not in favour of establishing an Islamic state. He astutely manoeuvred the support of the members in the Constituent Assembly to dilute the proposals of religious leaders. He involved his people to analyse other revolutionary ideas while assuring that he will protect religious interests of the Indonesian people. Panchasila became the Preamble of the 1945 constitution and equal status was offered to five religions. This was disliked by Muslim clergies who continued to grumble. Though the downfall of Sukarno is attributed to several factors but one of them was the opposition of important Islamic groups. They were critical of his socialist rhetorics, land reforms and dependence on communist forces. His successor, General Suharto, initially cultivated the religious groups and indulged in *Jehad* of the communists, but did not do anything to alter the constitution to suit their demands. The Muslim groups remained suppressed and ultimately felt cheated. They gradually started supporting Nahdlatul Ulama and Muhammadiyah to fulfil their interests. These organisations subsequently became vocal critics of the Suharto regime, which forced Suharto to counter them at the organisation level. He thus supported his information and technology minister, B.J. Habibie to float ICMI (Ikatam Cendikiawan Muslim Indonesia) in 1990.

The objective of ICMI was to develop awareness and understanding of Islam in all aspects of life. Habibie said: "ICMI is not a political organisation. Its main objective is to make a real contribution to the ever-increasing challenges to the way of life of the whole Indonesian population, especially the Islamic community".[17] Notwithstanding the government patronage, ICMI became controversial. The main Muslim organisations viewed it as an instrument of the government, bent on relieving the role of Islam in Indonesian politics.[18] They proved right and subsequently when Suharto resigned in 1998, ICMI lost its appeal. However the reality is that Suharto felt the need to cultivate religious groups in order to survive politically underlines the importance of religion in contemporary politics of Indonesia.

The President, Abdurrahman Wahid's survival in politics also depended on management of support of the religious groups. Though educated and trained in Pesantren and supported by Nahdlatul Ulama, he could not handle the politics of the country astutely. Again the unrest in Aceh and Irian Jaya on religious grounds could not be resolved. East Timor became independent because of differences between Islam and Christianity, but neither Suharto nor Habibie was a religious leader to be blamed. Wahid was a religious leader and therefore the level of expectations for conflict resolution on religious issue was higher. He did not display anything new to resolve ethnic disturbances either. He could not keep satisfied his partners, especially the Golkar, on whose support he had assumed Presidency. Hence Golkar changed its side to support Megawati and Wahid was forced to resign. Indonesia is on the democratic path and it is not easy to harmonise religion with development, stability and secularism to the satisfaction of all its citizens. It is a fact that Indonesians believe in mysticism and nobody can stop its impact at the community level. How it will evolve and affect the system, the leadership and broader politics are unpredictable. However, it is important to attend the grievances of the people necessary for the stability and prosperity of the nation.

## References


1. Satyavati Jhaveri, The Presidency in Indonesia: Dilemmas of Democracy, Bombay, 1975, p.39.
2. "Religion in Indonesia", Indonesia, New Delhi, Indonesian Embassy, 1998, pp. 64-65.
3. *Ibid.*
4. Indonesia in Brief, Information and Cultural Section, Embassy of the Republic of Indonesia, New Delhi, 1995, p.8.
5. D G E Hall, A History of Southeast Asia, London, 1968, p.47.
6. *Ibid.*, p.48.
7. Clifford Geertz, The Religion of Java, New York, 1969, pp.124-125.
8. Hendra Lapusa Awaludin, Bali Plus, Bali Denpasar, 1997, pp.6-7.
9. Anders *Uhlin*, Indonesia and the Third Wave of Democratisation, Richmond, 1997, p.64 and also see Cederroth, Survival and Profit in Rural Java, Richmond, 1995, p.230.
10. Indonesia in Brief, Indonesian Embassy, New Delhi, 1995, p.7.
11. Mutalib Hussein, Islam and Ethnicity in Malay Politics, Singapore, 1990.

12. Hassan Langgulung, "Philosophy of Islamic Education: The Indonesian and Malaysian Experience" in Hussain Mutalib, ed., Fazar Islam, vol.2. Singapore, 1989, pp.71-72.
13. Zainah Anwar., Islamic Revivalism in Malaysia, Petaling Jaya, Pelanduk, 1987, p.74.
14. Nawaz B. Mody, Indonesia under Suharto, New Delhi, 1987, p.152.
15. For details, see, Zuhri, K.H. Saifuddin, The History of Islamic Resurgence and Development in Indonesia, Bandung, 1979.
16. For better analysis of this aspect, see, Noer Deliar, The Modernist Muslim Movement in Indonesia, 1900-1942, Kuala Lumpur 1973.
17. Adam Schwartz, A Nation in Waiting, Indonesia in the 1990s, Melbourne, 1994, p.179.
18. *Ibid.*

# 4

# Ethnic Scenario in Indonesia

As stated earlier, the threat to the Republic of Indonesia is projected on the basis of ethnic turmoil in Aceh, Ambon and Irian Jaya, but there are some other islands also which demand greater autonomy on the basis of different language, history, religion or race.

Factional discontents have been brewing ever since independence, recent disturbances in different provinces have started with new vigour with the fragmentation of East Timor from the country in 1999. East Timor was the only area of Indonesia which had been ruled by Portugal. On the other hand Aceh, Ambon and Irian Jaya, etc. were the Dutch administered territories. East Timor was integrated by the use of the Armed Forces on geo-strategic considerations. It was neither acceptable to Portugal nor the United Nations and hence they provided moral support to the rebels. Indonesian leaders were unable to justify their intervention and this annexation remained controversial for decades. In order to understand this problem and its connection with Aceh, Ambon and Irian Jaya, it is in order to analyse the genesis of the crisis.

## East Timor

Situated in the middle of Indonesia and Australia and rich in gold, copper and sandal wood, the indigenous people of East Timor are of Melanesian descent. Their religion, customs and traditions are different even in comparison to the people in West Timor. It is quite well known that Timor Island was divided in 1859 whereby East Timor was ruled by Portugal and West Timor by Holland. West Timor became the integral part of Indonesia in

1945 but the question of East Timor remained unresolved till 1974.

On 25 April 1974, the Portuguese military overthrew the civilian government in Portugal, and the military, under the leadership of General Antonio-de-Spinola, took the control of the country. Less than a month later, President Spinola declared that democratic rights would be accorded to the inhabitants of the Portuguese colonies in Africa and Asia, including East Timor. The then Portuguese Governor and military commander, Colonel Fernando Alves Aldela, accordingly gave permission to the people of East Timor on 28 May 1974 to set up political parties and open the process that was necessary to hold referendum. As East Timor was surrounded by Indonesian territory, Indonesia started taking interests in the developments. It was in that year that Portugal decided to send Colonel Lemos Pires as a new Governor to succeed Colonel Aldela and pave the path for peaceful transfer of power in East Timor. Portuguese administration began to evolve ways and means for conducting the act of self-determination and in the process offered one of the three choices to be opted for the people of East Timor. They were the following:

(i) continuing association with Portugal,
(ii) integration with Indonesia, or
(iii) complete independence.

It was on these lines that three political parties emerged, *i.e*, Uniao Democratica Timorese (U.D.T) for continuing association with Portugal, Associacao Popular Democratica Timorense (Apodeti) for association with Indonesia, and Frente Revolucionario de Timor Leste Independence (Fretilin) for complete independence. The three parties had different goals and they had little co-ordination amongst themselves. They tried to establish their dominance and thus they fought against each other. Though the Portuguese offered alternatives to Timorese people to decide their future, they also fuelled seeds of discord and unrest. The situation became fluid and it was difficult to understand their real motive. As that territory is contiguous to

Indonesia, any major socio-political transformation in East Timor was bound to have implications on the politics of Indonesia. It was believed that an unfriendly regime in East Timor could disturb the security system of Indonesia and thus this area was projected as a "soft underbelly" of the latter. They supported the idea of integration of East Timor with Indonesia.

Ali Murtopo, then deputy chief of the State Intelligence Co-ordination Agency (BAKIN), supported the drive for mobilisation of domestic and international support in right earnest for integration. He was successful at the domestic front to convince the military leaders about the importance of East Timor for the security and political stability of Indonesia. He and his colleagues at the Centre for strategic studies advocated that the safest alternative for East Timor was integration with Indonesia. If they had chosen to opt for independence, it would have had destabilising impact because independent but economically unviable East Timor would be a satellite of the major powers. They also emphasised that the integration endeavour had the support of the people of Indonesia and particularly the chieftains of the two parts of Timor. As the intermarriage of the people between East and West Timor were permitted by the colonial rulers, they had family links. They supported the drive for integration. Osorio Soares, a respected leader of Apodeti, was a great protagonist of integration and under his leadership, there were some demonstration in Dili in support of Indonesia. He even paid a visit to the governor of Nusa Tenggara Timur to campaign for integration. There were some leaders who advocated that the Catholic establishment were also supporting the idea of integration with Indonesia because an independent East Timor was likely to be closer to the communist powers in the region. All these developments had positive impact in creating a near consensus that Indonesia should make attempts towards integration.

Indonesian leaders were not successful in advocating its case of integration internationally. Though Ali Murtopo supported by his colleagues from the centre for strategic studies undertook trips to the western world, Australia and the ASEAN countries. This exercise did not evoke the desired response, yet they made an attempt to create world opinion for their endeavours. Foreign Minister, Adam Malik met his Portuguese counterpart, Mario Soares in New York and conveyed to him the Indonesian opinion regarding East Timor and the latter gave assurance that they would try to accommodate Indonesian viewpoint. In July 1975, the Portuguese government ordered formation of a transitional government for the colony to prepare for election in October 1976 for a Popular Assembly that would take the responsibility of determining the future status of the territory. The transitional government was to be headed by a High Commissioner appointed by Portugal and five members - two Portuguese and three East Timorese. The Indonesian government proposed to Portugal for the formation of a joint Authority comprising representatives of Australia, Indonesia, Portugal and Malaysia to administer the need for a joint military task force to crush fighting and establish peace and order. However, these suggestions were ignored.

Fretilin, under the leadership of Ramos Horta, on the other hand, had different viewpoint, which was just an antithesis of what Indonesia was advocating. They campaigned for independence on ethnic and religious grounds and declared one force, one guide and one aim to gain independence. Jill Jolliffe has explained that "Fretilin leaders constantly stressed confidence in their belief that no matter to which party they claim allegiance, the followers must ultimately be 'Oan Timor', true children of Timore". Fretilin leaders thus tried to arouse ethnic sentiments and exhorted them to fight untidily against the dominance of the ethnic Malays (Indonesians). They also tried to mobilise support at the international level and sent their spokesmen to Portugal, Australia, China and some other countries. But the issues that proved irritating for Indonesia and some political parties of East Timor was Fretilin's growing liason with the Chinese and its leftist ideologies. An understanding of the socio-economic system of Timorese people, who are of Melanesian stock, makes it clear that the chiefs occupied special power and position in that society. Their roles were bound to be undermined within the communist or leftist order. They were thus opposed to Fretilin activities and some of them were seeking alternative political order to safeguard their interests. They were influential politically as the developments in Fiji (1987) have established.

It is necessary to have the understanding and good will of the native chiefs in a society dominated by the Melanesians to implement any reform or undertake any political experiment. The chiefs are obeyed by the ethnic population in that locality and in order to get the consent of the people for a movement, it is necessary to get the consent of the chiefs in the beginning. In case of East Timor, Fretilin aroused the spectre of nationalisation and socialistic drives, and they did not give proper attention to mobilise the support of the native chiefs. In contrast, UDT and Apodeti tried to mobilise the support of the chieftains in the beginning and were placed in a better position to be victorious in the event of referendum. But the situation became fluid and perplexing when the colonial masters adopted a fluctuating stand and the political contestants tried to establish their preponderance over each other with the help of brutal force and violence. Demonstration became the order of the day in Dili, and law and order situation worsened. Portuguese Governor found East Timor unsafe and strife-torn and therefore he preferred to stay at Atauro or Macao. His frequent absence from Dili intensified the conflict and ended up in a civil war.

At the outset of the civil war, UDT forces were in strong position and had the capacity to dictate terms. Its supporters had seized key installations, including the airport in Dili. It had also seized police headquarters and kidnapped the police chief in Dili. UDT leaders demanded imprisonment for Fretilin forces. Such a demand was not acceptable to Portugal. It was unwilling to do anything to offend the Fretilin.

In the meanwhile, there was polarisation of the political forces. UDT and Apodeti came closer to each other to take the support of the Indonesians and faced, untidily the challenge of Fretilin. Two other parties which had emerged in 1975—Kota and Partido Trabalhista—also supported pro-Indonesian parties and accelerated anti-Portugal and anti-Fretilin crusades. They had high-level meetings with Indonesian officials in Jakarta and Kupang respectively. UDT, under the leadership of Sr Fransisco Xavier Lopez da Cruz, announced thereafter that they would soon take action against Fretilin. He said: "We are realists. If we want to be independent, we must follow the Indonesian political line, otherwise it would be independence only for a week or a month".[1]

These developments alarmed Portugal. It sent Major Antonio Soares, a special envoy from Lisbon, to investigate the situation and find out solutions. He faced a grim scenario in East Timor. It was reported that clashes between the UDT and Fretilin had worsened. Fretilin guerrillas were using primitive weapons such as bows and arrows in their fight against the adversaries and thus hundreds had been killed. Fretilin had mounted campaign to regain the initiative and violent situation prevailed in Dili. Portuguese authorities in the territory admitted that they had lost control of the situation and appealed for international intervention to stop further bloodshed.[2] In the meanwhile Portugal decided to evacuate entire staff of the administration to Atauro. On the other hand, Fretilin troops were bombarding Dili by mortar fire. The situation became so tense that the people from East Timor began to leave their homes and seek refuge in West Timor. About 50,000 refugees had crossed the border to take shelter in Indonesia and hundreds were waiting at the border.[3]

These developments annoyed anti-Fretilin organisations of East Timor. In the meanwhile the strength of Fretilin forces were getting stronger who claimed to have control of Dili. There were strong repercussions in Jakarta over the Fretilin activities in East Timor. Indonesian Defence Ministry warned on 7 September that Indonesia would consider making pre-emptive strikes against Fretilin positions if they advanced closer to the Indonesian border. It alleged that the departing Portuguese were manoeuvring the situation so that Fretilin could take-over. (However Portuguese Timor must come to Indonesia for its national security as well as to avert regional instability). The official Indonesian news agency, Antara, raised the spectre of communism in Timor. It referred to hate-Indonesian campaign in East Timor and the move to impose communism with the support of colonial masters. Antara added further that the young Portuguese officials who were assigned the task of self-determination in East Timor, were members of the "Moviemento Forces Armada" and communist in Portugal. They went to the extent of saying that the Governor, Lemon Pires, was a member of the "Moviemento" and a communist party member.[4] Indonesian army newspaper, Berita Yudha, alleged that not only left-leaning Portuguese soldiers but also other foreign personalities were helping the Fretilin guerrillas. It came with an idea to counter it by arming the refugees from East Timor and sending them to fight the Fretilin forces.[5] While the strategists were coming out with ideas, Foreign Minister Adam Malik gave a clear warning that his country would intervene the moment the situation in the region posed a danger to its own territory. Now the foreign ministry took a position that the Indonesian nationalist leaders had always regarded the liberation of Timor from Portuguese colonialism and its integration with Indonesia was an extension of their own freedom struggle. They were determined now to forestall any possibility for East Timor to become a base for the revival of the battered Indonesian communists.

Fretilin did not give much attention to Indonesian sensitivities and tried to strengthen its foothold even before the act of self-determination that Portugal was to conduct. They proclaimed East Timor's independence on 28 November and asked Portugal to recognise it. Portugal, however, rejected the Fretilin pronouncement and instead decided to refer the case of decolonisation of East Timor to the UN. But it was too late to restrain the contestants. All the parties opposed to Fretilin—

UDT, Apodeti, Kota, and Partido Trabalhista—held a meeting at Balibo on 9 November to decide about their future strategies. They jointly issued their proclamation in the name of the people of Portuguese Timor to liberate themselves from colonial rule and expressed their determination to integrate with Indonesia.[6] It had an electrifying impact on the political developments. Adam Malik immediately flew to Dili to prepare the action plan. As a result Indonesia in coalition with UDT and Apodeti, decided to send its forces to establish order and peace in East Timor. The fighting started in the first week of December and it was over on 7 December, 1975. It is reported that Indonesia sent 1000 paratroopers and 4000 regulars, and they fought side by side with thousands of UDT & Apodeti volunteers.[7] Thus Fretilin forces were crushed and a new order was established. In this operation about 450 Indonesian soldiers were killed but Fretilin losses and casualties were enormous. They took refuge in deep forests and vowed to fight. Jakarta radio announced that Dili had been liberated by the people's resistance, spearheaded by Apodeti, UDT, Kota and Trabalhista and supported by Indonesian volunteers at the request of the people of East Timor with the support of Indonesian parliament[8]. As a result, a provisional government of the four coalition was established on 17 December, headed by Sr. Arnaldo dos Rais Araujo, as its chief executive officer. His tasks were to determine the organisational structure of the government and the responsibilities of its officers, and to define its policy, which aimed to restore social normalcy, integrate the territory into Indonesia, and adopt necessary laws and regulations. Indonesian Foreign Ministry subsequently announced on 21 March 1976 that the East Timor Provisional government had decided to establish their parliament to approve the merger of the territory with Indonesia and that the UN had been informed accordingly. Thus their House of Representatives which was known as People's Representative Council (PRC) was constituted with the membership of 28 leaders. They comprised one representative from Dili, 13 representatives from districts and 14 representatives from social and religious communities. On 31 May, PRC approved a petition to integrate East Timor with Indonesia. Besides UN, 25 other countries had been invited by Indonesia to observe this historic moment. Nevertheless observers came only from seven countries, *i.e.* India, Iran, Malaysia, New Zealand, Nigeria, Saudi Arabia and Thailand. The UN refused to send its observer and so was the case with other western countries.

Indeed Portugal, China and Australia initially opposed Indonesian stand on East Timor and contributed in internationalising it. They tried to influence world opinion against Indonesia. On the other hand, Indonesia tried to establish a strong grip in East Timor and tried to annihilate the opposition with a heavy hand. Fretilin, which displayed resistance, were outlawed. There was a great search for the rebels, and if traced, were put behind bars or killed. Times of India had reported on 4 June 1976 that more than 100,000 people—one sixth of the East Timorese population—had been killed in the aftermath of 1975. However Adam Malik refuted it and said that only 5000 to 8000 people were dead during that period. These aspects of life in East Timor were highlighted by Portugal and given adverse interpretation.

Indonesian officials subsequently indulged in excessive use of force. On 12 November 1991, Indonesian security forces fired at some demonstrators at Santa Cruz cemetery. Though the officials alleged that the demonstrators provoked the security forces and that the protestors were armed but the scrutiny of the developments refuted the official allegations. It was found out that the demonstrators had assembled at the Santa Cruz cemetery, to go to the Governor's office to present their charter of demands and they were peaceful. The security forces, which had banned demonstrations in the city, became suspicious about the motives of the large number of people assembled at one place. They tried to disperse them and in the process there were scuffles. As a result the security forces resorted to firing in which 115 persons were killed.[9]

This event was disliked at the national as well as international level. President Suharto ordered the formation of an investigation commission—National Committee of Enquiry—to enquire the causes of the incident and find out the persons involved in the Crime. A National Committee of Enquiry, chaired by the Supreme Court judge and members from the department of Home, Foreign and Justice Affairs, Armed Forces Headquarters, Parliament and Supreme Advisory Council was formed to conduct a thorough investigation.[10] Indonesian government officials expressed deep regret for the incident at the highest level and conveyed their determination to act firmly and swiftly to obtain the facts through a due legal process, and punish those held accountable for having violated the law, whether on the part of the demonstrators or the security personnel.

Portugal was most vocal against the firing at the Santa Cruz cemetery and ridiculed the formation of enquiry commission of Indonesia. In the capacity of Chairman of the European Community, Portugal raised the issue of human rights and self determination in East Timor. It appealed to the EC to stop economic aid to Indonesia and Holland expressed its willingness to do so. Portugal President, Mario Soares, during his official visit to India in January 1992 discussed East Timor with Indian counterparts. He tried to explain the problem of East Timorese people and demanded that the UN team should enquire the violations of human rights.[11] Portugal also tried to send a team of European Parliamentary members to visit Indonesia to enquire about human rights abuses and meet all sections of the people in Indonesia, including those from East Timor.[12] These delegations continued to come, but it was very difficult to bring about mutual understanding. The agitation against the government after 1992 was sporadic and it was over only after independence in 1999.

East Timor remained with Indonesia till Suharto was in power. His protege, Habibie announced referendum but he lost control over its details. On the other hand, the timing of the announcement was not favourable. Indonesia was in the grip of financial crisis and grappling with the unrest in different parts of the country. The referendum was held in East Timor in August 1999 amidst unprecedented violence and bloodshed. The people had two choices—either to prefer independence, or autonomy under Indonesian Republic. Ninety five per cent of the 390,000 voters gave their preference for independence. After East Timor became independent, it was the turn of Aceh, Ambon and Irian Jaya to demand referendum for autonomy.

## Aceh

Aceh is bounded on the north by the Malacca strait, on the West by the Indian Ocean, on the South and East, North Sumatra and Malacca straits. It has 97.5 per cent Muslims, 1.6 per cent Protestants and the remaining are Roman Catholics, Hindus, Buddhists and others.

The Acehnese have reputation of being religious extremists and they have till today, been pursuing an Aceh independence movement to achieve "*Aceh Merdeka*" (freedom for Aceh). As Aceh was the first part of the archipelago to be converted to Islam, it is the bedrock of Islamic religion and the Islamic faith which is practised with unusual intensity and severity in this part of Indonesia. It is the only place in Indonesia where a visitor can see women wearing full veils in *Kampong* (village). A man was caught stealing an old tape recorder and as a punishment, his hand was cut off in public. It is the same kind of Islamic law practised in Saudi Arabia and other orthodox Muslim countries that the people of Aceh prefer to pursue.

There are 3 million Acehnese divided into the earlier Pro-Malay hill people, the Gayo, the Alas and the more recent lowland coastal people who are a product of centuries of inter-racial breeding with the Batak, Dravidians, North Indians, Javanese, Arabs, Chinese and Nisans. The heterogeneous coastal Acehnese are taller, more stout and darker than most other Sumatrans because they are of Arabian, Indian, and Portuguese descent.

The Acehnese are real fighters. They are a people who seldom speak loudly and rarely point fingers at others. Despite the area's reputation for aggressiveness, most of them speak softly, always accompanied by gentle gestures. The younger generation shows respect for the older generation and always addresses the elders as *bapa* (father) or *ibu* (mother). Laughter is part of the Acehnese life for they love the sound of laughter. The region is known for its frequent festivals which include the water festival which is similar to that of the Burmese.

When Sukarno declared independence for Indonesia, the Darul Islam movement based in West Java attempted to establish a theocratic state in Indonesia. The Acehnese joined the rebellion and it took them many years (from 1953 to 1961) to come to terms with the central government which realised that Aceh was a political and not a military problem and made concessions to Aceh, including the establishment of the province of Aceh in December 1956, granting special status in mid-1959, agreeing to the application of Islamic law in Aceh in 1962 and offering an amnesty to Acehnese rebels. Today it is still a very sensitive area politically. Jakarta treats the Acehnese with arrogance and has declared Aceh a "special autonomous territory" (Daerah Istimewa) where Islamic law applies.

In December 1976, Tengku Hasan di Tiro, one of the Acehnese leaders of the Aceh Independence Movement (*Gerakan Aceh Merdeka*—GAM) under Daud Beureueh's leadership returned from the United States. Hasan di Tiro had been the self-appointed ambassador for the movement in the US and had on several occasions claimed the US had proffered support for the Acehnese rebels. Hasan di Tiro's attempts for new movement, however, failed to ignite the support of the Indonesian Muslims as it was aimed to secure independence for Aceh and possible union with the Federation of Malaysia. When it became known that Daud Beureueh had signed a proclamation in May 1977 calling for a holy war of independence from Indonesia, he was exiled to Jakarta. The GAM movement was crushed by 1978 and Hasan di Tiro went into self-imposed exile in Sweden and continued to speak against the government of Indonesia. He succeeded in mobilising some Acehnese for the impending war, but that was not sufficient to impress Suharto regime. In 1980, Acehnese youths began to receive military training in Libya. It was planned that 800 youths would be sent to Libya for training but ultimately only 49 went in the beginning. New militias began to prepare themselves for the war with the government. In 1988 an Indonesian territorial military commander was shot in the Pidie district. When in September 1989 a rebel military camp in Pidie was attacked and 20 weapons seized, the Indonesian government realised that rebels were reignited. The rebels portrayed themselves as revolutionaries who wanted to establish an independent Islamic Republic of Aceh. They highlighted the social gap between non-Acehnese engaged in oil, paper and fertiliser projects and they were prosperous. The central government was exploiting the resources and did not return a fair share of oil royalties to the Acehnese. The government at the same time was determined to crush the movement with a heavy hand. One rebel military commander was sentenced to death in absentia in September 1993 for burning a military headquarter, stealing 20 weapons, killing a number of Arabic personnel and evicting Javanese from transmigration sites.

For suppression of the Aceh rebellion, President Suharto sent 6,000 reinforcement troops including special forces, marines to wipe out the rebellion. The suppression produced quick results forcing the rebels to leave the villages and break into small guerrilla bands which became increasingly isolated from the population. Due to that operation, *Abri* had killed at least 2,000 unarmed civilians in Aceh by 1993. Hasan di Tiro remained safely in exile in Sweden but his local representative was shot dead in December 1992 and the rebels' military commander fled overseas. The conflict continued and there was unrest in the province. A number of Acehnese died and it was this reason that the Defence Minister and Commander-in-Chief of the Armed Forces General Wironto, visited North Sumatra on 7 August, 1998 to investigate reports of torture and killings during the past decade of crackdowns against separatist insurgencies. He announced that the troops would be withdrawn over the next month. General Wironto said, “On behalf of Indonesia’s armed forces, I apologise to the people of Aceh if, during military operations, the armed forces have made you suffer”.

The Legal Aid Foundation in Banda Aceh revealed that 10 mass graves had been found at three sites in the province, where the armed forces suppressed a separatist insurgency that peaked in the early 90s. The graves are believed to contain the bodies of hundreds of people killed by soldiers during operation “Red Net” which was carried out mainly between 1991 and 1993 to smash the insurgency and scatter its leaders. Acehnese are fighting for an independent Aceh but ground realities suggest that there is no consensus on this matter at the national level.

## Ambon

Bordered in the north by the Pacific Ocean, in the South by East Timor, in the West by North Sulawesi and in the east by Irian Jaya, Ambon has sizeable number of Christians. Protestants and Catholics comprise about half of the population known as Moluccans in the historical past, and have more than 150 dialects.

The word “Ambon” means “dew” in Indonesian. The island is almost always covered by fog or mist. That is what some people think “Ambon” is derived from. Another theory says the name comes from the word apon, which means plantation. In Ambon’s long history of exploitation, commerce has always been handled by outsiders, beginning with the Chinese, then the Arabs followed by the Europeans and now Indonesians.

Whatever the origin may be, Ambon has now become world famous because hundreds of thousands of Ambonese were repatriated to Holland after the pro-Dutch Ambonese failed in their attempt to establish a Republic of Maluku Selatan (RMS) and secede from Indonesia when the Javanese republican forces came to replace the Dutch colonial army. As a result of this repatriation, there are more Ambonese living in Holland than in Ambon.

The Abonese, numbering about 100,000 occupy 777 square km of land together with Hanruki, Saparua and Nusa Laut in central Maluku. They live on this island which was at crossroads since Dutch times. The Ambonese have mixed racially with the Portuguese, Alfuros, Malays, Javanese and Dutch, creating a sort of lighter-skinned coastal villagers. The interior people have darker complexion and more pronounced Melanesian features. The urban population has stronger Melanesian elements as people from surrounding islands flock to Ambon for jobs. The Ambonese speak a dialect classified as belonging to the Ambon-Timor group of Malayo-Polynesian languages.

Most Ambonese believe that their ancestors either hail from West Seram or at least spent enough time here to adopt its language and customs. They are basically divided into two groups—the Patasiwa and the Patalima. All villagers fall into one of these groupings and the *Adat* depends on the different circumstances in the founding of the villages. The two groups trace their origins to either east or west of the Mala River in Seram. Pata means "group" and Siwa means "nine", thus Patasiwa means group of nine (few know the significance of the figure nine, whether it is a group of nine or the distance from the river). Similarly, Patalima means group of lima, meaning five.

In 1871 when the Dutch colonised this island, they provided education to the Ambonese Christians who were hardly found in other parts of Indonesia, except the Javanese aristocracy and the Christians of Manado (north *Sulawesi*). As a result, the Ambonese threw in their lot with their colonial masters, even to the point of learning the Dutch language. They even imitated their Dutch masters in dress and conduct. They dubbed their first political organisation "Ambonese Wilhelmina Society" in honour of the Dutch Queen.

The most important segment of the Ambonese exodus, however, joined the Dutch colonial army which prior to World War II had integrated thousands of Ambonese soldiers. The Ambonese, like the *Gurkha* of the British Army, who were from

Nepal, were famous for their martial skills. They had fought with the Dutch as early as 1667 under Captain Jonkers and Admiral Speelman, and helped to defeat the forces of Makassar on Sulawesi. Ambonese also staffed the force for vicious hongi expeditions which enforced the spice monopoly and fought with the Dutch in the bloody 1675-1682 Java wars. During the Dutch colonial period, the Ambon*ese* were a class of their own. They were the "Black Dutch" carrying out the orders of the Dutch to suppress rebellions within Indonesia. They made ideal soldiers: smart, brave, tough, obedient and respectful. During the early part of the 20th century, the Ambonese made up half of the colonial army and were crucial to the military expeditions that brought many semi-independent areas under Dutch control. Some of the Christian Ambonese identified themselves so closely with the Dutch that they referred to their island as the 12th province of the Netherlands.

Special status for the Ambonese was the hallmark of the Dutch colonial policy. The Dutch needed them and therefore provided them comfort and education until they were completely Dutch-oriented. Ambonese liked to be addressed "Black Dutch" and were proud of the new name. They had found no common ground with the Indonesians in general and therefore were critical against Indonesian regime, especially the Javanese, on the eve of independence. Ambonese treated Indonesian government as their new master trying to control them. Thus the entire background was not propitious for healthy relations and integration. The activities of Ambonese overseas fuelled fire and sporadic skirmishes continued. But they intensified their struggle in 1988 and it is a matter of great concern to the government.

## Irian Jaya

Irian Jaya is bordered by the Pacific Ocean in the North, Arafura Sea in the South, Papua New Guinea in the East and Ambon in the West. This province inhabits 59 per cent Protestests and 24 per cent Catholic Christians, and has been in the limelight ever since 1945. The Dutch colonial masters did not hand over this area to Indonesia along with other islands, but there were intense struggle for more than a decade wherein the United Nations resolved it by accepting Indonesian claims in 1963. This island has several tribal groups of which Dhanis and Biaks are important. Dhanis are divided into several clans and most of them still continue with their stone age life style. But when the Dutch left, they had prepared the ground for guerrilla warfare for self-determination. Furthermore, there was large scale rigging of the polls of the 'Act of Free Choice' which was already predetermined.[13] The coastal Papuans by early 1960s adopted a national flag, anthem and coat of arms to fight for Papua Merdeka under the leadership of Organisasi Papua Merdeka (OPM).[14]

Since then there has been cyclical bouts of ethnic assertion for independence and expressed in the form of raising their morning star flag. In 1970's and 80's they resorted to attacks on oil installations and oil tanks, kidnapping Indonesian officials. Though it is undoubtedly the creation of the Dutch, OPM's intensification for Merdeka has also to do with Indonesia's policies. Dr. Mochtar Kusumaatmadja, the then Indonesia's Foreign Minister at a state banquet asserted his PNG hosts that Indonesia did not want to retain Irian Jaya as a zoo.[15] Such attitude of looking down on the Papuans and impending cultural dominance of alien people made them feel alienated from the mainstream. One such assertion of cultural rights was 'Operasi Koetka' named after 'Kotekas' or penis shealts worn by traditional West Irianese men.[16] These traditions are regarded tribal and disliked, but *Papuans* feel that it is an essential part of their culture.

The educated Papuans took asylum in the Netherlands and have since then been fighting for their homeland with little success. Another major cause for resentment by indigenous people is the transmigration policy of Jakarta mainly from over-populated region of Java to West Papua. Inter-ethnic conflicts and control of fertile land by outsiders is a cause of concern to the local population.[17] Many of the Papuans fled and took refuge on the other side of Papua New Guinea (PNG). The Melanesian brothers of PNG sympathise with Irianese (Papuans) though PNG government recognises West Papua as integral part of the Republic of Indonesia.[18] This helps the OPM to take sanctuary across the PNG-Indonesian border and operate it from there.[19]

Moreover, there is dominance of outsiders in official, administrative and economic spheres over the less educated and primitive people. Another important dimension of ethnicity which is gaining ground is the exploitation of resources. One of the country's largest mining area at Tembagapura alone account for 30 per cent of Indonesia's export but there is little investment and West Papua has lagged behind other provinces because of formidable terrain and extremely limited infrastructure. OPM activities target the exploitation sites and the villagers often clash with the companies. Another source of disgruntlement is uncontrolled intensive fish exploitation including illegal use of explosives which has depleted the environment and fish reserves of Jayapura and Sorong.[20]

Indonesia has reviewed its policy and is working hard towards fostering communication links by building 800 km. long Jayapura-Merauke road along the Papua New Guinea Border which is yet to be completed. New emphasis like 'parallel development' for environment protection and not forcing the indigenous people to move over to wet rice farming has been on its agenda. Another important policy is its encouragement of dialogue with the secessionist Free Papua Movement.[21] Jakarta has allowed Irian Jaya to change its name to West Papua to appease the people. The OPM at any time, if becomes a strong viable movement, may prove a disturbing factor for the central government of Indonesia.

## OPM Structure

Some of the Dutch educated nationalists took up political asylum in the Netherlands and also on the other side of PNG. They constitute a significant proportion of Papuan nationalism and have been fighting for their homeland through propaganda and political activities. Those Netherlands based OPM founders like Nicolas Jouwe and Marcus Kaisiepo were from Arafak island. Their unit was called the Papuan National Front (FPN) from which the name OPM (Organisiasi Papua Merdeka) was derived.[22]

OPM has a flag (featuring morning star of Biak island), the national symbol of the crested pigeon, the anthem 'O, My Land of Papua, and 129 articles of the Provisional Constitution of West Papua which is printed in a blue booklet.[23]

The Free Papua Movements military arm (papenal) or Pasukan Pembebasan Nasional (National Liberation Force) is organised into seven regional commands, each one consisting of a large number of posts known as basis.[24] Each regional command has 1000 to 3000 trained guerrilla attached to it. A significant proportion of troops is also comprised of women cadres.

The OPM lacks modern weapons and its weaponry include bows, arrows, spears and long sharp cassowary bones.[25] Most of its fire arms are World War II vintages. Another source of its arms are guns seized from Indonesian army. They also lack medicine and trained medical personnel. One advantage of the OPM against the Indonesian Army is that they have a thorough knowledge of the jungle. The OPM functions like a government, with posts such as defence, finance, home and foreign affairs, information education and local government.

In areas where they have a control, they provide basic training for medical treatment, give attention to education and organisation of food production etc.[26] However, the organisation is characterised by factionalism which sometimes leads to infighting among the groups. Leaders of such factional groups often fight for leadership of the OPM (Free Papua Movement). They also do not have clear ideology.[27] There is also split between the rival groups over method of fighting the Indonesian government—one group prefers armed opposition and the other prefers 'dialogue' as a means of achieving West Papuan's Independence.[28]

In its integrative process of West Irian (West Papua) with the mainstream, Indonesian Government in collaboration with the army undertook formidable task of developing the territory with energy and dedication. Priority was given to road building as a means of access to the interior and control of the population. Another major task of the Jakarta Government was to provide an energetic programme of primary and secondary school education. Development funds have been earmarked from Dutch (FUNDI)[29] and Indonesian sources. Indonesia also continued the Indonesianisation process in all government, cultural and educational institutions.

The people of West Papua are Melanesians who are ethnically similar to the rest of Papuans who inhibit the other side of New Guinea *i.e.* Papua New Guinea and the indigenous people of the Solomon Islands, Vanuatu, New Caledonia and Fiji. Out of the five million people (Melanesians) who live in the Asia Pacific region, one million of them are in West Papua. West Papuans have not only close ethnic relation but they also have common Melanesian way of life and culture.

To conclude, it can be stated that ethnic dissection of the Indonesians displays thousands of ethnic groups and their life-style varies from one another. Indonesian leaders therefore evolved the concept of "Unity in diversity". However the economic development in Indonesia has not yet percolated down amongst the weaker sections of the society. Since the basic needs of the people are not fulfilled, they are unhappy with the system. If their unhappy state of affairs are exploited by their new leaders with malafide intentions, if they are exhorted to be united in the name of race, religion and ethnicity, and if the emerging group gets trans-national support to create disturbances, the conflict is accentuated. There are evidences that Libya and Saudi Arabia have been ardent supporters of the Muslim fundamentalists. On the other hand, Christians have been supporting their co-religionists in Indonesia. There arc several instances to support this in case of East Timor, Ambon and Irian Jaya. The state was intolerant of dissident activities under the military rule and therefore the spectre of colonial rule could not be avoided. The end of the Suharto era, however, gave birth to problems in the realm of economic development, social harmony and Panchasila philosophy. The call for *Jehad* by the militants and revenge for the *Jehadis* in some parts of the country have jolted institutions supporting "Unity in diversity".

## References

1. Keesing's Contemporary Archives, Bristol, 23 January 1976, p.27533.
2. *Ibid.*
3. J. Soedjati Djiwandono, "Indonesia's Security Concerns and Responses", Journal of Asiatic Studies, vol.27, 1984, pp.227-38.
4. Times of India, New Delhi, 27 March 1975.
5. Times of India, 3 January 1998.
6. Facts on East Timor, House of Representatives of the Republic of Indonesia, 1990, p.13.
7. Keesing's Contemporary Archives, 23 January 1976, p.27534.
8. *Ibid.*, p.27535.
9. Times of India, 13 & 15 November 1991.
10. News From Indonesia, Embassy of the Republic of Indonesia in India, New Delhi, 20 November 1991, p.1.
11. Hindustan Times, New Delhi, 20 November 1991.
12. Times of India, 28 January 1992.
13. National flag featuring morning star and national anthem, Hai Tanahku Papual (Hai Papua our Motherland) and coat of arms featuring (crown dove).
14. Peter Hastings—National Integration in Indonesia, the case of Irian Jaya in "Lim Joo - Jock and Vanis", Armed Separatism in South East Asia (Published by Institute of Southeast Asian studies, Singapore, 1984), p.129.
15. *Ibid.*
16. Chris Manning 'Far Eastern Economic Review', 30 April 1987, p.40
17. Ibid, p.11.
18. *Ibid.*, p.11.
19. *See* 'Far Eastern Economic Review', 30 April 1987, pp.40-42.
20. John Haseman, "Indonesia Plans Irian Jaya Talks" Asia Pacific, 18 November 1998,
21. Malcolm Gault Williams, "OPM: The Free Papua Movement Lives". Bulletin of concemed Asian Scholars, Vol.9, no.4 Oct. Dc. 1987, p.35.

22. R. Osborne, "Indonesia's Secret War, the Guerrilla Struggle in Irian Jaya, London: Allen and Unwin, 1988.
23. *Ibid.*, p.37.
24. *Ibid.*
25. Osborne, No. 22, p.56.

# 5

# Politics in Indonesia

Political developments in Indonesia have more similarities with India than any other country in the world, but their perception about each other have been changing from friendly to hostile to normal. When Sukarno advocated the organisation of New Emerging Forces (NEFOS) and confrontasi, India was unhappy. Similarly when Indira Gandhi advocated support for separatist movement in Pakistan and the creation of Bangladesh, Indonesians were annoyed. The concept of confrontasi was counter productive and the creation of Bangladesh changed the political contours of the region, the impact of which are yet to be resolved. The aim of this paper is however to analyse briefly the developments in politics of Indonesia from 1945 to 2001.

As mentioned earlier, post-independence era in Indonesia had been dominated by two Presidents, namely Sukarno (1945-1965) and Suharto (1965-1998) respectively. Both had taken active part in the independence struggle and both proved towering personality amidst their adversaries. Both had their strong points and weaknesses. Whereas Sukarno, like a visionary, wanted to evolve a new world order in which the role of the Western World had been minimised, Suharto emphasised on economic development at the domestic level. Sukarno was charismatic in influencing public opinion, but came under the influence of the communists (PKI) which led to his downfall. On the other hand, Suharto was authoritarian but developmental. He came under the impact of his cronies and family members in decision making, which led to his downfall. An analysis of the role of Sukarno and Suharto in Indonesian politics are sufficient in order to understand Indonesian politics, but a little reference to nationalist movement would be in order for a proper perspective.

## Nationalist Movement

Although anti-Dutch sentiments existed in Indonesia ever since the beginning of colonial rule, but their articulation was slow and gradual. It is a reality that Prince Trunojoyo of Madura fought against the Dutch in 1680 and was martyred. There was a revolt against the Dutch colonial rule under the leadership of Pattimura in the Moluccas in 1816-1818. Again Prince Diponegoro of *Mataram* (Java) fought a fierce battle against the Dutch in 1825-30. Another nationalist, Tunku Imam Bonjol of West Sumatra and Tunku Umar of North Sumatra led a revolt against the Dutch during 1873 to 1903. King Udayana of Bali had fought against the Dutch colonial forces in 1908 and similarly there are many other instances in which the Indonesians fought for their identity and independence. Nevertheless all such events were projected as incidents due to the failure of law and order. All these events had been organised at a regional level, in which there was no co-ordination at the national level. The situation started changing with the formation of Boedi Oetomo on 20 May 1908, which under the leadership of Dr. Soetomo, was apparently established for educational reforms but it was aimed at arousing the people against the colonial rule. Dr. Soetomo was inspired by Japan's Victory over Russia in 1904-05 and believed that if the people in Indonesia too are mobilised, they can repeat the performance of Japan against the Dutch. This organisation had all-Indonesia character and it expanded its activities at the national level.

Boedi Oetomo generated enthusiasm amongst the nationalist forces, and subsequently a number of nationalist parties came into existence. H.O.S. Tjokroaminoto and Haji Agoes Salim established Sarekat Islam and K.H. Akhmad Dahlan formed Muhammadiyah in 1912, followed by the formation of Partai Indonesia by Douwes Dekker, Tjipto Mangunkusumo and K.H. Dewantoro for independence of the country. In 1927, P.N.I (Indonesian Nationalist Party) were born. Both P.K.I and P.N.I accelerated the struggle for independence. They adopted a militant policy of non-co-operation with the government and pledged their allegiance to "one country, one nation and one language Bahasa Indonesia".[1] Their activities were complimented by Indonesian youth organisations which were earlier known as young Java, young Sumatra and young Ambon merged with one another. They undertook several programmes for social awareness and insurrection and the Dutch colonial masters were alarmed. The Dutch rulers jailed, exiled and killed several nationalists but they could not suppress the momentum for freedom struggle.

The nationalist movement in Indonesia were solidly supported by Japan during the Second World War. Japan defeated the Dutch colonial forces and installed Sukarno as the President of Indonesia. It was with the support of the Japanese that the civil administration of the country came into the hands of the Indonesians, and Indonesia Raya was recognised as the national anthem and Bahasa Indonesia was accepted as the national language. The Japanese demolished the concept of white supremacy and allowed the nationalist forces to operate freely in the country. The Japanese propagated "Asia for the Asians", and complete eradication of Western influence, culture and prestige in the region. Indonesia complimented Japanese efforts by popularising three slogans:

(a) Japan the leader of Asia,

(b) Japan the Protector of Asia, and

(c) Japan the light of Asia.

These slogans indeed proved useful in gaining the confidence of the Japanese but the nationalist leaders in Indonesia, by agreement, worked in two directions while promoting the nationalist cause. One group, headed by Sukarno and *Hatta* collaborated with the Japanese, and another headed by *Sjahrir* and *Sjarifuddin* went underground to organise a resistance movement. It is understood that both groups had an understanding of each other's activities and they worked for Indonesian insurrection and independence. Thus we find that national and international developments helped Indonesia to be victorious in the war for independence. Indonesian leaders generated forces for insurrection and revolt all over the country to the extent that it was impossible for the colonial forces to re-establish themselves, but they unlike India did not wait for the colonial masters to announce decolonisation. They, on the eve of the impending defeat of the Japanese, proclaimed their independence on 17 August 1945. When the Dutch tried to come back, the resistance war started. At the same time, Indonesian question was referred to the United Nations. The police action of the Dutch and dialogues at the UN continued from 1945 to 1949. President Sukarno claimed sovereignty over the entire archipelago, but the Dutch did not agree to concede. In order to overwhelm the nationalist force, the Dutch military attacked Yogyakarta in December 1948 and arrested Sukarno, Hatta and many others. They were detained at Bangka, off the east coast of Sumatra, from where they escaped with due assistance from India. The Dutch action was openly criticised by India and Australia and this issue was raised at the UN Security council, which adopted a resolution for a cease-fire, release of detained leaders and peaceful settlement of the conflict. Finally the Round Table conference was organised in the Hague on 23 August 1949 under the auspices of the UN and the decision was that Holland should recognise the sovereignty of Indonesia. Thus the Dutch recognised the freedom and sovereignty of Indonesia on 27 December 1949.

## Sukarno Period

Although Mahatma Gandhi led the freedom movement in India, he could not lead the nation in the post independence era. On the other hand, Sukarno led the freedom movement and the government in the post-independence era. As a visionary, he had certain ideals about the socio-economic life of his people. As an Indonesian nationalist he was impressed with the glories of the

Majapahit empire, which had united most of the islands into a single entity in the name of Dwipantara. King Hayam Wuruk with his able Premier Gajah Mada (1331-1380) had expanded the frontiers of the country and their reign have been projected as the golden period of Indonesia by the historians. Champa, Cambodia, Siam and Burma had accepted the domination of the Majapahit rulers as described in Negara Kertagama of Prapanch. Most of the territories of present day Southeast Asia comprised the territories of the Majapahit rulers.

Sukarno had astute knowledge of Indonesian history and social realities. He was regarded as father of the nation and therefore he wanted to abridge the gap between the rich and poor. He supported the policy of nationalisation of the Dutch enterprises to bring them under indigenous control and promote the policy of one language, one nation and common nationalism. In order to dilute separatist tendencies on different islands, he promoted the concept of "archipelagic outlook" which meant the following:

1. The realisation of the Indonesian Archipelago as one political unity, in the sense:
   (a) that the entire territory of the nation with all its people and resources forms one territorial unity, one place, one sphere of life and one set of norms of all the people, and is the asset and property of the nation;
   (b) that the Indonesian nation, consisting of various ethnic groups and speaking a variety of regional languages, following a variety of religions and faiths and worshipping God in various ways, form one complete national unity in the broadest sense of the word;
   (c) that psychologically, the Indonesian people should have a sense of belonging, having one destiny, and one sense of responsibility, of being one nation with one motherland, imbued with a strong determination to achieve the national ideals;

(d) that Panchasila is the only philosophy and ideology of the state and nation, whose basis is to guide and direct the nation towards its goal;

(e) that the entire Indonesian Archipelago forms one legal unity in the sense, that there shall only be one national legal system serving the national interest.

2. The realisation of the Indonesian Archipelago as one social and cultural unity, in the sense:

   (a) that the Indonesian society is one and lives in the pursuit of equal, widespread and balanced social progress in such a manner that life is in harmony and follows the advancement of the people;

   (b) that the Indonesian culture is essentially one, whereas the various forms are only a reflection of the cultural wealth of the people which is a fundamental asset for national cultural development to benefit the people.

3. The realisation of the Indonesian Archipelago as one economic unity, in the sense:

   (a) that the potential and real resources in the territory of the Archipelago, are the collective asset, the property of the people, and that the daily necessities of the people must be provided equitably throughout the country;

   (b) that the stages of economic development in all regions should be even and balanced without disregard to the specific characteristics of the regions in improving their economic life.

4. The realisation of the Indonesian Archipelago as one unity of defence and security, in the sense:

   (a) that a threat to any island or region is in effect a threat to the entire nation and state;

   (b) that every citizen shall have equal rights and duties regarding the defence of the country and the people.

Sukarno's archipelagic outlook had geopolitical implications. His claims of sovereignty, according to archipelagic outlook, was not confined to the Dutch administered territories. He claimed sovereignty rights over British Malaya, and Brunei as well. Projected widely as the tallest leader of the Malay world, he believed himself to be the natural leader of the ethnic Malays, whether they inhabited at Java, Mindanao, Patani, Malaya or Brunei. Thus his concept of archipelagic outlook had trans-national implications, which generated tension and conflict. Sukarno's crush Malaysia plan and his support to Azhahari-led insurrection in Brunei spoiled his international reputation. He was projected as reckless and irresponsible leader jeopardising international peace and stability. His actions created a panic situation in the region and thus five-power-defence-pact was organised to provide security cover to Malaysia and Singapore. Thus the indulgence of great powers in the power politics of the region grew. Sukarno had used the appeal of race, language and history to boost the feeling of nationalism, but his statements regarding Malaysia proved counterproductive. The parallel may be drawn in case of India where the leaders talked abut their culture and influence in "further India", encompassing Cambodia, Pagan, Siam, Malaya, Java and Sumatra to promote their feeling of nationalism. Southeast Asian intellectuals were unhappy with such projections and argued that their culture and civilisation are indigenous, that they are not the components of further India and also that India should be watched carefully. In retrospect, we find that India respected the sovereignty of Southeast Asian nations but in order to generate nationalist feeling it was necessary to glorify its history and civilisation, and extent of its impacts on Southeast Asia. The Dutch, the French, the British and the German scholars had given a feed back about prevailing Indian culture in Southeast Asia in the 18th and 19th centuries and Indian leaders and intellectuals interpreted them in their own way. They never intended to denigrate history and culture of Southeast Asians, but the impression was not favourable. Similarly Sukarno had never intended to offend the bonds of fraternity in the Malay World, but inadvertently committed some errors, which proved one of the causes of his downfall.

Another contribution of Sukarno was the concept of guided democracy based on historical and cultural realities of Indonesia. He did not believe in the adoption of Western concept of democracy as followed in the Great Britain or the United States. He believed that Asian countries faced different problems distinct from one another, and to cope with they needed indigenous political system. Their democracy has to reflect their own socio-economic realities. The division of powers, fundamental rights, freedom of the press, political parties and media, etc., should be complimentary to the goal of common nationhood and nationalism. They should look for guidance towards the chief executive (Presidency) and should not do anything to disturb national goals. President Sukarno had endeavoured to evolve a new concept of democracy, known as Konsepsi. He believed that there are many obstacles in Indonesian culture and social system that make the functioning of Western type of democracy—based on adult franchise, direct election and party system—difficult to operate. A relationship is yet to be established between the vote and advanced technology. It was argued that the peasant civilisation of Asia cannot easily imbibe the complex values on which modern governments in Europe and the US are based. The social and political traditions of rural population are oriented towards allegiance to personal authority rather than obedience to the rule of law.[2] The political parties have no means and no opportunity to provide proper political education to the masses. The guided democracy was to take cognisance of the socio-political realities of Indonesia and offer a vibrant and effective political system.

President Sukarno declared a proclamation of emergency in March 1957 and hence the cabinet started functioning under the direction of the President. The President, as the head of state, and supreme commander of the armed forces, assumed all the powers of the government on 9 May 1957. The President issued an emergency act to establish a national council. The function of the council was to render advice to the government on matters of state *i.e.* social, political, military, economic and financial matters. The creation of the national council had been necessitated "in the further development of state life". Other means (besides the legislature) were still needed for the channelization of the growth of those forces in the community which were steadily moving and could not be properly channelised through the existing means.[3] The establishment of the National council was also justified on the ground that it would help in mobilising the forces in the community to help the government in its welfare programmes. It was hinted that the political party system and the House of Representatives (DPR) working under that system were inadequate to deal with the teething troubles of the new Republic. The members of the National Council were to be appointed from regional leaders, military and civil authorities.

Sukarno was determined to bring about socio-economic transformation but the then religious and regional leaders smelt foul in the emerging scenario. They began to organise opposition to the government policies and the demand for creation of Islamic state was accelerated. Sukarno could not handle the rising opposition under the existing framework and apparently subverted the democratic processes. On 5 July 1959, he took a landmark decision to dissolve the Constituent Assembly which had almost drafted a new constitution. The democratic ethos that had been evolved through 1949 and 1950 constitutions were done away with and 1945 constitution was restored.

The Presidential decree of 5 July 1959 recommended the reinstatement of the 1945 constitution. All the powers of the government were given in the hands of the President and the post of the Prime Minister was abolished. This return to the political system adopted immediately after the proclamation of independence was defended on the ground that 1945 constitution reflected the true spirit as demanded for the nation. The spirit to be promoted on the eve of independence—the spirit of unity, Musyawarah and Mufakat were necessary to be promoted for nation building. It was presumed that with the revival of this spirit, Indonesia would resume its onward march towards a society based on Indonesian ideals, in which people would enjoy the material prosperity and spiritual regeneration.[4]

Whatever the compulsions and motivations for adopting guided democracy, it did not yield the desired results. With the restoration of 1945 constitution all the members of the MPR were appointed by the President. On the other hand, DPR was also dissolved and a new one appointed to represent three major political streams, namely the nationalist, religious and communist groupings. Again he filled judiciary also with appointed members.

Thus the powers of the three branches of government was made subservient to the Presidency. The members of the M.P.R. (People's Consultative Assembly) acted not only as a rubber stamp, but proved their bankruptcy by appointing President Sukarno, as a President for life. Such a decision was disliked even by those Indonesians who liked Sukarno as father of the nation. The period of guided democracy in Indonesia may be compared with the declaration of emergency in India (1975-77). Although the emergency had been declared to promote socio-economic life of the Indians, it became unpopular and retrogressive. Sanjay Gandhi, the second son of Prime Minister Indira Gandhi, started dominating the political scene. He undertook demolition drives and forced family planning arbitrarily. There were unrest in all parts of the country and thus the emergency had to be withdrawn. In case of Indonesia, the Communist PKI became the collaborator of Sukarno in the period of guided democracy (1957-65) and started implementing land reforms and socialistic goals arbitrarily. The communist factor proved a liability for the leadership of Sukarno, and consequently the army take-over was the resultant conclusion.

Another contribution of Sukarno was his efforts towards consolidating solidarity of the third world based on anti-Western rhetorics. He opposed the containment drive of the United States and the formation of Southeast Asia Treaty organisation (SEATO). He organised Bandung conference in 1955 in which 24 Asian and African countries participated. The purpose of the conference was to promote closer and amiable co-operation in the economic, cultural and political fields. The resolution adopted was known as the *Dasa Sila* of *Bandung* to strive for world peace, to promote respect for each other's sovereignty and territorial integrity, and non-interference in each other's internal affairs. The resolution sought to uphold the universal declaration of human rights. Sukarno was one of the founders of the non-aligned movement which was launched in 1961. However, the subsequent developments indicated that he was solidly backing the socialist block and socialist agenda. He started giving preference to the Soviet Union, People's Republic of China, Democratic Republic of Vietnam, Cambodia, North Korea and Cuba in foreign policy matters. He was enunciating radical views against the Western World which proved confrontational. In this way, Sukarno offended not only the Western World but also the opinion of the neighbouring countries. Although, Sukarno tried to gain economic sovereignty for the third world, it was not realistic. However his opinion is still remembered. Presently, whatever is happening in Malaysia and whenever, Mahathir Mohammad confronts the Western World on the question of human rights and economic exploitation, parallel is drawn of the Sukarno era. It is a fact that the third world provides the raw material to the Western world and it continues to remain a market, as it was during the colonial period. There is still the lack of advanced technology. There was nothing wrong if Sukarno tried to articulate this point through international forums. In this sphere he worked as a catalyst to consolidate the opinion of the third world. He excelled better than Nehru or any of his contemporaries, while highlighting the problem of exploitation of the Afro-Asian World by the colonial powers.

## Suharto Period

On 30 September 1965, P.K.I. attempted a *coup d'etat* under the leadership of Aidit, Untung and Subandrio. They arrested six army generals and captured a radio station. They killed the generals and dumped them in an abandoned well on the outskirts of Jakarta. This provoked retaliation of the armed forces. Thus the army in Jakarta under Suharto started counter offensive very effectively. Suharto had the backing of the military and others who opposed communism in Indonesia. The communist forces could not withstand the army onslaughts and therefore army take-over was smooth. But it was not easy to get rid of Sukarno, who was still the most popular of all the leaders. So the students were prompted for general strike and demonstrations. They demanded *Tritura* (three points), namely, to ban the PKI, to replace Sukarno's cabinet and to reduce the prices of basic necessities. On the other hand, public was also encouraged to hold a street parliament to articulate their opinion against PKI and views against Sukarno. The subsequent developments convinced Sukarno to accede power to Suharto formally on 11 March 1966 and hence the era of new order ushered in and Suharto became the *de facto* President. Suharto is credited to lead anti-communist crusades. He ordered the search for communists and thousands of PKI members were arrested and killed. The members of those organisations, who were affiliated to P.K.I. were also detained. More than half a million people were arrested or detained.[5] According to Robert Scribb about 500,000 PKI members and sympathisers out of the estimated three million members were killed and 1.5 million detained.[6] The military commanders had the authority to arrest people for political reasons and there was no legal protection to challenge the arrest. P.K.I. members, sympathisers, suspected sympathisers and innocents were made the targets of the persecution.[7]

Another contribution of Suharto was the evolution of *dwifungsi* (dual functions) of the armed forces. Besides the security of the country, the armed forces were promoted in civil administration and politics of the country. The role of the armed forces in the freedom movement was highlighted and similarly their role in the nation building and modernisation were sought to be enhanced. Their contribution as social and political force were recognised. They were encouraged to take part in the national development. The armed forces thus launched the drives for development of the villages in line with the civic missions of the Armed Forces. They assisted the village population in the construction of roads, bridges and the irrigation system to promote the welfare of the rural community. Thus the armed forces strengthened their base at the grassroot level. The military were preferred as executives in the companies and they emerged the principal figures in the management of oil exploration and mining. *Dwifungsi* also implied that the head of state in Indonesia would be selected from the armed forces. Suharto supported this principle till it suited his leadership, but when he sensed that there was a challenge to his leadership within the armed forces, he overlooked the ideals of *dwifungsi* and selected Habibie, a civilian, as the Vice-Presidential candidate in 1998. As Suharto was undergoing treatment for his failing health at that time, it was believed that Vice-President is bound to succeed him. As *Habibie* did not have a military background, the armed forces witnessed a *fait accompli*, in which they were forced to accept a civilian to be the President in the event of resignation or death of Suharto. The armed forces, that had been ruling the country since October 1965, became annoyed and their loyalty to Suharto became questionable. This was one of the major factors for his downfall. Had he honoured the principles of *dwifungsi* in letter and spirit, the situation might have been different.

Another contribution of Suharto was in the field of economic development. He evolved plans for economic rehabilitation in 1966 and signed agreements with some countries to reschedule an overseas debt of US $ 5 billion. Attempts were made to gain overseas credibility and in that endeavour he succeeded in the formation of a consortium of creditor countries to assist in its economic development. The consortium, known as Inter-governmental group on Indonesia comprised the US, Canada, Australia, New Zealand, Japan, Britain and some other European countries. The technocrats and economists, educated and trained in the US were promoted in the economic management and thus the external credibility of the government lost during the Sukarno period was resurrected. The new team for economic management, known as Berkeley Mafia astutely opened the system of centrally planned economy towards liberalisation and the decision proved rewarding. The growth rates recorded impressive gains and it was 6.3 per cent in 1979, 9.9 per cent in 1980 and 7.9 per cent in 1981.[8] In 1982, the growth rate came down but again it picked up momentum. In 1983 the growth rate was 4.2 per cent, in 1984 it was 6.1 per cent and in 1987 it was 3.6 per cent.[9] The growth rate increased to 7.34 per cent in 1994 and the performance showed that the growth rate was 6 to 7 per cent every year. This was impressive compared to Sukarno era, wherein it was merely 2.1 per cent. It is known that in 1965 the per capita income of Indonesia was $ 70, half that of Bangladesh and India. But it increased to US $ 884—triple that of Bangladesh and double that of India—in 1995-96. Foreign investment steadily increased and it was US $10 billion in 1992, US $ 8 billion in 1993, US $ 24 billion in 1994 US $ 20 billion in 1995 and US $ 39.7 billion in 1996.[10] Thus foreign exchange reserves grew to US $12.13 billion (excluding gold) in 1995 and export figures were high at US $39.7 billion compared to imports at 30.9 billion in 1994. Indonesians below the poverty line who comprised 60 per cent of the population in 1965 was down at 10 per cent in 1995 and the birth rate which was 5.5 per cent earlier was reduced to 2.4 per cent. There was significant rise in the number of middle income group during Suharto era and the economic management was admired by the IMF and World Bank. Thus Suharto symbolised an important pillar of development and stability in the region.

In retrospect we find that he altered the system of economic development pursued by Sukarno, but as far as the authoritarian political culture of the Sukarno era was concerned, attempts were made to institutionalise and promote it. After the signing of the super semar by Sukarno on 11 March 1966, Suharto became the acting President. He vowed to return to constitutional life initially and retained 1945 constitution for the governance of the country. He also upheld Panchasila as the state philosophy and ideology, so much so that his regime was projected as Panchasila democracy. He promised to hold general elections once in every five years and said that the MPR is supreme state institution and DPR should be an elected body and exercise control over the conduct of the government. The mechanism of control by the DPR was emphasised to prevent constitutional deviation and the demand for elected representatives were underlined to win popular support. But his performance subsequently showed that his regime was an improved version of guided democracy. Only difference was that Sukarno had communists to back up his administration but Suharto had the armed forces to support his regime. Sukarno tried to highlight Panchasila but Suharto stretched it further. As the official Handbook says, "Panchasila democracy means democracy based on people's sovereignty which is inspired by and integrated with other principles of Panchasila".[11] This meant that the use of democratic rights should always be in line with the sense of responsibility towards God almighty according to the respective faith, upholding human values in line with human dignity, which would guarantee and strengthen national unity, and aim at realising social justice for the whole people of Indonesia.[12] In simple words, the meaning and significance of Panchasila became so confusing that it was not easy for lawyers to define it. As understood by the general people, Panchasila meant obedience to superior authorities and President was its final interpreter.

Suharto suppressed all opposition and every challenge to his authority. He also banned political parties under the pretext of Panchasila democracy. Sukarno during 1957-65, had evolved the concept of *Nasakom* (*nasionalisme, agama dan Komunisme*) to curtail the activities of the opposition. The nationalism, religion and communism were highlighted to balance the rightist and leftist elements for his power politics. Suharto encouraged democratic elements initially and vowed to destroy *Nasakom*, but he gave birth to a new version of it in the name of *Naspika* (*nationalisme, spirituil dan Karya*) to crush the opposition. He promoted the union of nationalist, spiritual and functional groups in parliament aimed at reorganising the party system.[13] This gave birth to the formation of three groups in parliament, namely, Sekbar Golkar, the Indonesian Democratic party, and the Development Unity Party. Whether it was guided democracy or New Order, opposition to the government was curtailed. Opposition activities were not allowed and they were asked to obey the principles of Panchasila, the interpretation of which were in the institution of Presidency. Nawaz B. Mody, while analysing this aspect said that Suharto's policies were aimed at controlling political parties, ensuring their docility and preventing them from emerging as a threat to military rule.[14]

The conduct of foreign policies were more realistic as Suharto linked it with his domestic needs. The primary objectives of his foreign policy was the following:

(i) to support national development with priority in economic development as set out in five year develop ment plans;
(ii) to preserve internal and regional stability conducive to national development, and
(iii) to protect the territorial integrity of Indonesia.

Besides Suharto tried to normalise relations with neighbours, particularly Malaysia. The crush Malaysia Plan was abandoned and friendly gestures were exchanged. Indonesia's attempt to cultivate relations with neighbouring states helped in the creation of new regional grouping, known as Association of Southeast Asian Nations (ASEAN). This association, which became a Trojan house of success, had five members in 1967, but finally all the countries in Southeast Asia joined it for regional co-operation. The ASEAN boom continued till Indonesia showed stability and development and Suharto intended to be projected its Chief architect. The MPR resolution regarding ASEAN in 1988 stated that co-operation among the public and private sectors of ASEAN member countries should be intensified with a special emphasis on economic, social and cultural co-operation.

This, in turn, would reinforce the national resilience of each member country and the regional resilience of ASEAN, thus enhancing the common endeavour to build a Southeast Asian ZOPFAN.[15] Indonesia assumed major role in the conflict resolution at the regional level. It organised Jakarta cocktails to resolve conflict in Cambodia and contributed its share in the peace process. It also organised several workshops on South China sea to resolve the contest for overlapping sovereignty claims over the Spratlys. However, it failed to handle the dispute in East Timor satisfactorily. In 1975, when the armed forces occupied East Timor, it satisfied the nationalist aspirations of the Javanese and enhanced the legitimacy of the military rulers as this had helped the territorial expansion of existing boundaries. However when this issue was raised at the UN, Indonesia could not argue its case convincingly. Whether it was Adam Malik or Mochtar Kusumatmadja or Ali Alatas, they could not justify Indonesian intervention in East Timor because that was the obligation of the UN to resolve. The case of decolonisation had been referred to the UN by the former colonial master (Portugal) on the eve of Indonesian intervention and it was extremely ambitious on the part of Indonesia to force its solution without assessing its global repercussions.

The plan for the conquest of East Timor, called operasi Komodo, was directed by Ali Murtopo, who tried to create international opinion for Indonesian claims. However, Bapak Sukarno, who claimed Irian Jaya, Malaya or Brunei, had never raised the issue of East Timor. But now the issue of decolonisation was raised and the legitimacy for military intervention was advocated. Indonesia had West Timor (*Nusa Tenggara*) under its sovereignty because it was the Dutch administered territory. Now they wanted East Timor on historical and geo-political grounds. The Indonesian leaders tried to impress that its intervention was natural and also that its occupation was necessary for its security. They also claimed that Timor island was Indonesian territory during Srivijaya and

Majapahit periods and geographically this island fell within the archipelagic claims.

The military rulers, who had indulged in the *Jehad* of communist forces were apprehensive of communist activities in the region. They were reportedly unhappy that Fretilin leaders were interacting with Communist China and if East Timor is ruled by Fretilin, it would certainly be under communist influence. There were a number of Indonesian communists in China in exile and the projection was that they would treat East Timor as a base to export revolution to Indonesia.

Indonesia wanted to prevent such eventualities and therefore they made an alliance with two major political parties of East Timor, namely, Timor Democratic union and Apodeti, and sent its security forces. The campaign was brief and effective. The island was occupied and declared the 27th province of Indonesia. Portugal protested against Indonesian actions and raised the issue at the UN. Indonesian action in East Timor became controversial. Fretilin continued to oppose integration with Indonesia and intermittent war continued. This issue was brought into international focus repeatedly but when B.J. Habibie became the President, he called for a referendum, and the result was separation of East Timor from Indonesia as a sovereign independent state in 1999. This development had massive repercussions on other provinces demanding autonomy or independence.

Indonesia could not handle the problem of financial crisis also which initially started in Thailand and Korea in July 1997 and reached Indonesia. Though President Suharto felt great concern, he was unable to tackle it satisfactorily. He became increasingly dependent on IMF to resolve the crisis and accepted the reform agenda. He distanced himself from the economists who had been the pillars of his success since 1966. He removed the governor of Bank Indonesia and sought advice elsewhere. When he was re-appointed the President in 1998, most of the advice tendered by IMF was implemented, except the establishment of currency board system as advised by Professor

Steve Hanke of Johns Hopkins University. Suharto felt that IMF programme by itself was not going to resolve the problem because when he signed an agreement with the IMF on 15 January, the Rupiah had lost another 40 per cent of its value. With a total depreciation of some 80 per cent, the private sector of the economy was bankrupt.[16]

Suharto was most anxious at this juncture about the inflationary effects due to the devalued currency which could not be resuscitated. There were rough estimates that if the currency stayed at the 10000 - 12000 level against US $1, inflation would build up over 200 to 300 per cent over a year.[17] When there was already rioting over price rise and shortages, the question was what would happen if prices doubled and kept on going up while more businesses packed up and household incomes shrank. Indonesia had presented a case of market failure, where there was a massive flight of capital goods and foreign currencies. As a result, Jakarta stock exchange collapsed. There were unforeseen fall in the value of the Rupiah, and rapidity of the capital flight was traumatic. The availability of the foreign currency became scarce and the banking system failed. Sixteen banks were closed and the work on many foreign sponsored projects were stopped. The IMF came out with certain new conditions to provide bail-out funds and tension was visible at the socio-economic level.

There was growing criticism that as far as IMF reform measures were concerned, Indonesia was not taking the right steps. The IMF started saying that Indonesia should treat Thailand and Korea as models to cope with economic crisis and restore confidence of the international market. With the deterioration of economic and political order, the leadership of Suharto was questioned at the internal and external level. The economic development, which his regime symbolised ever since he came into power, became so weak that it posed a major threat and cause of unrest. The US and the IMF which had been the strong supporters of the regime, became critical. They projected Suharto himself a problem, under whose leadership a satisfactory agreement was unlikely to be workable.[18] Thus slowly and steadily the agenda for democratisation was propagated. It was argued that under Suharto's leadership, it was difficult to restore market confidence in Indonesia or stabilisation of currency and a resolution of the private short-term debt issue. The US media and the congress started highlighting the issues of nepotism, corruption, human rights, labour laws and the massacres in East Timor and Aceh. All these issues were linked with the economic crisis and powerful campaign was launched to dislodge President Suharto. On the other hand, Suharto also did not display statesmanship when he selected a civilian to be his Vice-President without taking into confidence the opinion of the armed forces. This worsened the situation in Indonesia where political demonstrations and anti-Chinese riots occurred intermittently.

In view of the growing unrest and communal riots and demonstration against him, President Suharto resigned and his Vice President, B.J. Habibie became the acting President in May 1998. His Presidency was not welcomed as he was the protégé of Suharto . Again Habibie was not from Java, where the majority of the Indonesians inhabit. He was from Sulawesi and identified with discredited Suharto. Thus anti-Suharto lobby continued to haunt him. He first tried to restore law and order and visited China Town to provide confidence and security to the ethnic Chinese who comprised three per cent of the population. He said that he would change the law to remove the differentiation between Pribumi and non-Pribumi, but his rhetoric and exhortations were not effective. As he was not from the armed forces, his opinion did not carry much weight in the armed forces. The communal riots became intensified after 13 May 1998 when the mobs shouting slogans started, saying, "Let us butcher the Chinese", "Let us kill the pig eaters" or "the Chinese pigs". The mobs threatened to castrate Chinese in Indonesia. About 5000 Chinese-owned buildings were burnt and several thousands killed. Their shops, warehouses and homes were looted and thus there was an exodus. The worst affected areas were Medan, Surabaya, Aceh, Solo and Ujung Pandang. Habibie did not succeed economically either. The Central Bureau of Statistics stated in 1998 that Gross domestic product (GDP) for the full year was to fall further by 13.6 per cent and GNP was to fall down to US $ 436 from US $1,055 in 1997. Most of the industrial plants were closed and 15 million people were out of work.[19]

Despite failures and a brief tenure, Habibie will be remembered in Indonesia for holding referendum in East Timor. Contrary to the spirit of musjawarah and gotong royong, like an autocrat, announced referendum without discussing the matter in the Cabinet or the DPR. Hence the United Nations came into the picture and thus Soli Sorabjee, envoy for the UN High Commissioner for Human rights visited East Timor. He evolved plans for surrender of arms from pro and anti-independence factions. The registration of voters started on 16 July 1999 for an estimated 390,000 eligible voters. The referendum was held on 30 August 1999 amidst violence and bloodshed. East Timorese were asked whether they would like to become independent or gain autonomy under Indonesian control. The counting indicated that the overwhelming number of people wanted independence.

Habibie will also be remembered for holding nation wide elections in June 1999 wherein 48 political parties contested. The monopoly of the Golkar Party was diluted and democratic ethos were given importance. Megawati Sukarnoputri's Democratic Party (PDI) got 33.74 per cent of the votes, followed by Golkar 22.44 per cent, National Awakening Party, 12.61 per cent and National Mandate Party 7.12 per cent. As the election of the President is conducted by an electoral college, the members of the MPR, there was much scope for manipulation. Golkar initially supported Habibie and felt that the smaller parties would support them. But this mobilisation proved ineffective. Megawati supporters thought that her party had the largest number of seats in the DPR, and had the support of Nahdlatul Ulama and so she was bound to be victorious. However when the elections were held, Abdurrahman Wahid emerged victorious as a result of clever manoecuring and statesmanship. There was a direct contest between Megawati and Wahid and the result showed that Wahid got 373 votes and Megawati got 313 only. As Golkar Party decided to back up Wahid at the end, it tilted the balance and Wahid was the winner with 54 per cent votes whereas Megawati received only 45 per cent votes.[20]

The new President came into power on 20 October 1999. Wahid's credentials as an effective leader was doubtful as he was nearly blind. He was therefore dependent on his inner circle for information and advice. It is understood that two daughters of the President, namely Alisa and Zannuba served as his eyes and ears. They read for him and interpreted the body languages of the people he talked to.

Wahid took the advice of his brothers namely Hasyim, Salehuddin and Umar for the statecraft. All this had adverse impact on his performance. Although projected as the son of the soil with lot of mystic powers, he could not prove successful. Being educated and trained in Pesantren (Islamic schools) and formerly the Chairman of the Nahdlatul Ulama with 30 million members, he had been renowned in upliftment of the community life for decades. But the problem of Indonesia today is how to move effectively on the development track and synchronise community life for harmony and peace. The national debt is US$ 134 billion or 83 per cent of the GDP.[21] The system demands prudent fiscal policies to cope with economic problems. There is a growing demand for decentralisation of revenues and power to the regions as separatist sentiments are felt in different provinces. The law and order situation have declined and crime rates and violence are increasing. The armed forces are also disgruntled and their display of factionalism have promoted the anarchic situation.

Wahid was unable to cope with challenges. Indonesia is a large country and its management problems are also very big. Wahid had little experience to govern in the past. His thoughts on leadership, public education and management was limited to Pesantren. In his book *A Pesantren Anthology* he wrote about issues in Islamic boarding schools. In his public statements, he called himself an educator or a teacher but as a President, he had to look after organisation, finance and management at the national level. Foreign investments were not coming. From October 2000 to April 2001, there were approval for just US$ 1.9 billion foreign investments. The value of Indonesian Rupiah was down to 8685 per US $. It was 20 per cent lower than the existing figure in 1998, and the total government debt swelled from 23 per cent of the GDP in 1997 to 83 per cent in 1999.[22] The banking system had to be resurrected and a new spirit to infuse strong faith in the unity of the nation was demanded. His government did not perform as per the expectations, and thus the unrest continued.

President Wahid became increasingly isolated in power politics. His blindness, poor health and above all some corruption charges made him unpopular and the legislature (MPR) was convened for questioning the President on 23rd July 2001. President Wahid adamantly refused to face the proceedings and hence party impeachment was initiated against him. Golkar which had supported Wahid's candidature for Presidency, was now vocal against him. Besides Golkar, 593 members of the MPR supported impeachment proceedings which started on 23rd July 2001. President Wahid tried to impose emergency and dismiss the legislature. He even appointed a new police chief officer, but all efforts failed, as there was total unanimity over his removal. MPR felt that the President had exceeded his authority by issuing a decree suspending the MPR and DPR and by declaring emergency. Wahid was charged for breaching the constitutional provisions. Amien Rais, the speaker of the DPR, who presided over the special session of MPR, announced the removal of Wahid from Presidency after the voting and appointment of Megawati in his place. Indonesian military and police also supported the dismissal of Wahid. Vice Admiral Ronggo Sunarso while endorsing the removal, welcomed the appointment of the new President. Hence Vice President

Megawati Sukarnoputri was chosen to lead the nation. She is secular in her approach, young and dynamic. She has better rapport with regional leaders and is expected to bring peace and prosperity to the nation.

Megawati has been a renowned activist in social, cultural and environmental areas. Being an undisputed leader of Indonesian Democratic Party (PDI), she has made all efforts and sacrifices for restoration of democracy and in this endeavour she enjoys grassroot support. However, the level of expectations are very high which is impossible to be fulfilled in near future.

Indonesia is facing problems of different types. The present political system and reforms are not satisfactory. The restructuring of democratic institutions are needed as reforms (Reformasi) are slow. Amien Rais, a popular leader, has been supporting the restructuring of three branches of government and trying to evolve the system of checks and balances. He is keen to see the legislature empowered enough to check and balance the Presidency in the event of crisis. The members of the MPR and DPR should be in a position to take independent stand on crucial matters. He also believes that the number of political parties should be limited in the Parliamentary elections. In 1999, the number of political parties contesting in the elections were 48, which is not good in keeping with the national ethos. In this context, MPR on 3 October 2000 decided that only those parties, who won more than 10 seats in the DPR in 1999 general elections would qualify for contest in the next general elections in 2004. It was also decided that the President should be summoned before the MPR to account for his performance on annual basis, to break the past practice of accountability after five years. Decision was taken that all the members of the House of Representatives (DPR) should be popularly elected and real power should be entrusted to the legislature so that it does not act as a rubber stamp.

Megawati has endorsed all these resolutions, but she is more concerned with the problem of management and development. Indonesia is limping back to normal condition after the financial crisis. The World Bank and the IMF have been demanding reforms for more democratisation and human rights as a condition to provide loans. Again the problems of corruption, omission and commission, which have been the legacy of the previous regimes, need to be tackled. The civil unrest and the demand for regional autonomy, financial allocation between the centre and the provinces and political relationship of regional administration with the centre also need to be rationalised. The stability of the government has to be maintained and development of the peripheral areas are to be focussed upon.

The substantial threat to the country is generated by ethnic disputes. Megawati has been telling that excessive ethnic pride poses a threat to national unity. If their demands are conceded, there is every possibility of Indonesia emerging as a Balkan. She has argued that "we often make a disproportionate use of ethnic or local symbols. I feel concerned when people use ethnic pride, 'local people' or even religious symbols to support the case of regional autonomy. The spirit of national unity formulated by the founding fathers would be transgressed if each region were to focus on pursuing their own interests".[23]

The new leadership indeed is trying to evolve a new national vision and strategy in keeping with the changing times. The President is trying to take advantage of her proximity with regional leaders and establish an effective grievance redressal mechanism. Being a leader of the coalition government, she has to enlist the co-operation and confidence of her partners. Although the magnitude of social, political, religious and economic problems are gigantic, and party lines are sharply divided, the government is bound to take care of them for national unity, harmony and lasting peace.

## References

1. Satyavati S. Jhaveri, The Presidency in Indonesia: Dilemmas of Democracy, Bombay Popular Prakashan, 1975, pp.241-42.
2. *Ibid.*, p.248.

3. For details see Republic of Indonesia, the Indonesian Revolution, Basic Documents and the Idea of Guided Democracy, Jakarta, 1961.
4. Amnesty International, Indonesia, An Amnesty International Report, 1977, London 1977, p. 15
5. Robert Scribb, "Indonesia", Far East and Australia, London, 1999, p. 416.
6. Nawaz B. Mody, Indonesia under Suharto, New Delhi, Sterling, 1987, p.180.
7. Indonesia 1989: An Official Handbook, p.115
8. *Ibid.*
9. *Ibid.*, 1994, p.81.
10. *Ibid.*, 1987, p.55.
11. *Ibid.*, 1987, p.55.
12. Resolution No.11/MPR/1988.
13. Rawson Dalrymple, "Indonesia and the IMF", Australian Journal of International Affairs, Vol. 52, No. 3, Deaking, November 1998, p.234.
14. *Ibid.*, pp.234-35.
15. *Ibid.*, p.236.
16. Lee Khoon Choy, A Fragile Nation: The Indonesian Crisis, Singapore, 1999.
17. Asia Week, 7th July 2000, p.29.
18. Asia Week, 7 July 2000, p.34.
19. News from Indonesia, New Delhi, October 2001, p.17.

# 6

# Terrorism – Blast in Bali

A new history of terror and bloodshed began in Indonesia after the fanatics of *Jemaah* Islam*iyah* (JI) bombed tourist resorts at Bali on 12 October 2002. The bombing of Kuta, Renon and Manado shook the international community and they were alarmed. The government of Indonesia recovering from the economic crisis and the problem of political instabilities (1998-2002), faced with a greater threat of Islamic terrorism. Bali blast caused the death of 190 and injuries to more than 300 people. Press statement accepted the death of 182 and injuries to 132 persons.[1] The Times of India reported the death of 187 and injuries to 300. Most of the victims were foreigners from Australia, Britain, France, Germany and Sweden. Almost half of them were from Australia but the other half were from Britain (30), France, Germany, Sweden and Indonesia.

Bali is regarded as a paradise on earth and world's most popular tourist destination. It attracts holidaymakers, jet setters and backpackers at global level. October bombing turned the throbbing strip of bars and discotheques into a scene of bloody carnage. There were two explosions at Kuta—a small one in the Paddy's discotheque—followed by a far more powerful one outside Sari. Another bomb went off 50 meters from the US consulate in Sanur, also a tourist spot.[2]

President Megawati Sukarnoputri felt traumatised and instantly flew to Bali to express her condolences. She said that Bali blasts were a warning that terrorism was a threat to national security. She inspected the site of the bombing and spoke in general terms about how terrorism violates the fundamental values of all religions. She, however, was not clear on how she and her government would tackle terrorism in Indonesia. Indonesian forces were instructed to beef up security around oil and gas installations particularly operated by foreign multinationals like Exxon Mobil, for fear of further terrorist attacks. Indonesian press statement on 13 October expressed condolences and deep sympathy to the bereaved families by reiterating that "Such a brutal and inhuman acts of violence contravenes laws, religious teachings and moral standards of Indonesian people".

British Prime Minister Tony Blair expressed his horrors and Australian Prime Minister, John Howard while expressing his frustration that Jakarta was the weakest link in the battle against Islamic militants, urged Indonesia to crack down on terrorists. Howard felt great concern about the carnage wherein hundreds of Australian tourists died. This was bound to have repercussions on Australian public opinion and thus Howard while expressing his anguish went a step further by threatening pre-emptive strikes against any country in the region, which Canberra saw as a base for an actual or potential terrorist attack. He defiantly asserted that Australia had the right to pre-emptive action.

The United States was equally concerned at the developments in Indonesia. It had been warning the Indonesian government in the past that a group linked to Al Qaida was planning to kill Americans and other Westerners but it was not given much attention. Ralph Boyce, the American ambassador in Jakarta had himself conveyed this information to top officials. The US had come to know about the operation through Omar al-Faruq, linked to terrorist group in Indonesia. It had been made clear that the attack would not necessarily have on official American site as its target, but also those areas, which attract American civilians. Ralph Boyce had spoken to Megawati "to wrap up the terrorist cells, block it and demonstrate that you are serious about eliminating the threat against us". Indeed the US signalled that Indonesia was a terrorist heaven after the carnage in Bali and ordered 350 Americans connected with the US Embassy—about 100 diplomats—to leave the country.[3]

The US denounced bombing by calling it a "despicable act of terror". It believed that Osama bin Laden's Al Qaida network was trying to establish a foothold in the world's most populous Muslim nation. Although none of the terrorist groups in Indonesia claimed responsibility for the bombing, but it was clear that the terrorists linked to Al Qaida had planned and executed the heineous crime at Kuta. The *Jemaah Islamiyah* is indeed responsible for the bombing. The Indonesian police for investigations summoned Abu Bakar Bashir, projected main suspect of the crime. Bashir was also summoned under an article in the criminal code on treason, which is theoretically punishable by death.[4] But his lawyers, Mahendradatta and Ahmad Khalid believed that summons against Bashir were not justified. Mahendradatta said, "We can only say that we are sad that the government has succumbed to international pressure to arrest *ustadz* (the teacher)."

The US and Australia subsequently circulated a report blaming *Jemaah Islamiyah* for deadly bombings and pleaded with the United Nations to declare *Jemaah Islamiyah*, a terrorist group. The US State Department added the group to its own list of terror groups on 23 October 2002. It was dedared that it would be a crime to contribute funds to *Jemaah Islamiyah*. The members of this terrorist group were debarred from entering the US. Both countries hoped that a UN Declaration would help them launch an international campaign to isolate it and cut its financial support. Singapore and Japan expressed solidarity with the Americans in approving the proposed declaration to support the campaign against terrorism in the region.

The UN Security Council on 14 October strongly condemned the attacks on Bali and urged the international community to work together and help Indonesia see that justice was done and the perpetrators punished swiftly. Reaffirming the need to combat terrorism in accordance with resolution 1373 (2001), the council unanimously adopted resolution 1438 which essentially calls for the Indonesian government to allow other countries to come and investigate the attack and combat terror by all means.

The intelligence document made available through CIA, details a confession made by Omar Faruq, regarded as bin Laden's envoy in Southeast Asia, who was arrested in Indonesia in June, and handed over to CIA subsequently. It revealed that Abu Bakar Bashir the spiritual leader of *Jemaah Islamiyah*, received $74,000 from bin Laden's account.[5] This amount was for purchase of explosives to be distributed to Islamist groups. Bashir was questioned for terrorism in relation to a series of bombing of Christian Churches, treason for plotting the assassination of Indonesian President, immigration offences and destruction of property. Faruq revealed a series of plots to kill Westerners, Indonesians and Israelis.

Indonesian police started looking for the culprits of the Bali bombing and came to know that Imam Samudra was the mastermind of the blast. He along with two of his body guards—Rauf and Yudi—were arrested. Indonesian Police Chief, Dai Bachtiar said that Samudra having six aliases, was a leading member of the *Jemaah Islamiyah*. He chaired meetings to plan the October 12 night-club terror bombing which killed 190 people, identified the targets and gave the order to carry it out. It was after the arrest of Samudra that the name of another terrorist came into the picture. Hambali, an Indonesian whose real name is Ridnan Isamuddin, is the chief of operations group of JI and is also believed to be a leading member of Osama bin Laden's *Al Qaida*. He has escaped to Pakistan, but is being wanted by five countries in Southeast Asia. He has been linked with terror operations in different countries of Southeast Asia. It is indeed very difficult to arrest the terrorists because they have meticulous network to escape. If Imam Samudra was arrested, credits must be given to a mobile phone technology operated by joint investigation team of Australian and other foreign agencies. Indonesian police arrested him aboard a bus that was about to cross the Sunda Straits by ferry to Sumatra.

It was only after Bali bloodshed that Indonesian government accepted possible link between local militants and *Al Qaida*. The administration used to deny any links of the terror groups with *Al Qaida* in the past and when Lee Kuan Yew said that Indonesia is a favourite ground of *Al Qaida* after September 9/11, there were hostile reactions in Indonesia. Many top officials expressed their disagreement with the observations of Lee Kuan Yew and Singapore was projected unfriendly. When an Indonesian General Hendropriyono said that *Al Qaida* agents were present in Indonesia, it was taken as a false information. Some leaders even demanded that Hendropriyono be dismissed from the services. When Paul Wolfowitz, Deputy Secretary of Defence in Washington said that after Afghanistan, the US target will be South Philippines, Malaysia and Indonesia, there were widespread reactions. The ideologues of radical Islam were angry with the observations of Wolfowitch. Their reaction was that Western "infidels" have conspired to tarnish Islam's image. Any demand to fight terrorism was criticised and projected as anti-Islamic. However, when Abu Bakar Bashir and Imam Samudra were arrested, it was clear that they had definite links with *Al Qaida*. The terrorist organisations have made an effort to divest regional reactions after Bali outrage by saying that the CIA is responsible for the blast because this could force the administration to crack down on Islamic groups.[6] There are many people who disagree with such rhetorics but at the same time there are some who attach importance to such observations.

The influence of Islamic groups are spreading and they are not neglected. Indeed they are increasingly used by politicians and ambitious leaders to promote their interests in power politics. They know very well that the terrorists propagate militant *Jehad* for the establishment of a theocratic state. They also know that Islamic radicals are striving for implementing *Shariat* laws against the existing constitution (1945) and drop *Panchasila* as the guiding principles of the state, yet they are trying to appease them to extract political advantages. The number of Islamic radicals may be small but their views are properly highlighted in the recent past because there are many who believe that Islamic terrorists are fighting for dignity of the Islamic people and for their resurgence. The fight against Western supremacy is their fundamental right, and the US and the Western world must be taught a lesson for their support to the zews against Arab Muslims. The US policy towards *Al Qaida*, Taliban and Saddam Hussain are projected as a threat directed against the Islamic World. The terrorists have supporters in the administration. Vice President, Hamzah Haz has openly supported radicals like Abu Bakar Bashir of JI and Jafar Umar Thalib of Laskar *Jehad* (LJ). He has been visiting pesantren (boarding schools) run by JI and LJ and delivering lectures to provide them legitimacy.[7]

Indonesian politicians are generally reluctant to publicly criticise the ideology and strategies of radical Islam. They do not want to be seen as un-Islamic as their eyes are fixed at coming general elections in 2004. They advocate that Islam is the only thing left in Indonesia to feel proud of. Islamic groups on the other hand, are trying to project Islamic religion as the most important element of Indonesian nationalism. They argue that if there is proper assertion of Islam, Indonesia will be the unquestioned leader of the Malay world. Sukarno had indeed envisioned the leadership role of Indonesia in the Malay world but his policies were disowned by his successors. Now those ideas are being resurrected in the framework of radical Islam. There are no leaders now to counter the ideology of terrorists, and presently most of the political leaders are grooming pressure groups based on religion to promote their electoral prospects.

This is not to suggest that the administration is not doing anything to cope with the threat of terrorism. When the trade towers had been bombed in New York, President Megawati had personally visited the US to express her concern and solidarity. She expressed co-operation in establishing an international front to tackle terrorism. Indonesia along with other ASEAN partners held a meeting with the US in New York to build a consensus to combat terrorism. Accordingly the partners agreed on three points of co-operation—the exchange of intelligence information, improvement of potential to deal with the question of terrorism and also to evolve mechanism against terrorist attacks.[8] Thai Prime Minister Thaksin Sinawatra later visited Indonesia and talked of concerted efforts to battle terrorism, including exchange of intelligence.[9] Hasan Wirajuda, Indonesian Minister of Foreign Affairs, spoke that the administration was ready to round up the terrorists and bring them to justice. He agreed to destroy their cells and their networks and deny them their ill-gotten financial and other resources. Let us see that there are no safe heavens anywhere for any of them.[10] Indonesia introduced anti-terrorism bill on 3 October 2002 which defines terrorism as an illegal act carried out intentionally that endangers people and their belongings or sparks widespread destruction, fear or causes death. Terrorism, therefore, can be directed to damage a range of targets, including national assets, the environment, state secrets, culture, education, the economy, technology and industry.[11]

The bill threatens terrorists with a minimum three years in jail and a maximum sentence of death. Capital punishment will also be imposed on terrorists who commit attacks using airplanes, or those who misuse chemical, biological or nuclear materials. Those who have the intention to carry out such attacks could be sentenced to a maximum of 15 years in jail.

Anyone who smuggles in and out of Indonesia or manufactures, receives, hides or uses weapons, ammunition or explosives with the intention to terrorise others will also face death. A company convicted of organising a terrorist act will be fined one trillion Rupiah (US $111 million) and will be dissolved and declared a banned organisation. The bill also says that investigators, prosecutors and judges can order banks to block and disclose accounts and other properties of suspected terrorists. While investigating terrorism, the bill stipulated that bank secrecy laws do not count.[12] These measures complimented the law about money laundering and ratification of the International Convention on the Suppression of Financing for terrorism, the convention against Trans-national crime and the convention on the Suppression of Terrorist Bombings ratified by the President of Indonesia in April 2002.

After the Bali blast, the government took vigorous steps to empower the police and security authorities to act more decisively to thwart terrorist activities. The President issued a Regulation on the eradication of terrorism and Presidential Instruction mandating the co-ordinating minister for political and security affairs to co-ordinate measures in combating terrorism, and another Presidential Institution giving the head of the National Security Agency the authority to co-ordinate all intelligence activities.[13]

Although various steps have been taken and mechanisms evolved to fight against terrorism, it is not regarded sufficient. The biggest problem with the present system in Indonesia is that whenever they pass any resolution, it is viewed as dictated either by the World Bank, IMF or the United States. In case of fight against terrorism also, the impression generated is that it is done with a view to appease the United States. The political leaders and the national media have failed to project the losses incurred due to terrorist activities. After the bomb blast in Bali, the country is projected as a failed state and the confidence of the foreign investors are losing.

It is understood that the cost of terrorist attacks are greater than September 11 attacks in the US (US $10 billion). Michael Schuman says that psychological shock waves surging outward from Kuta Beach are bound to intersect with the nation's fragile social and political ecosystem in unpredictable ways, testing the allegiances and resilience of an ineffective government, and dealing a body blow to a sputtering economy that has yet to fully recover from Asia's 1997 economic crisis. The bomb blast in Bali hurts a situation that is already bad.[14]

The business community has to cope with random violence. A bomb had earlier exploded in the building housing the Jakarta Stock Exchange, killing 15 people. But Bali blast is more serious. In the week following that blast, the US athletic gear giant Nike stopped ordering sneakers and thus a factory on the outskirts of Jakarta was closed. The country's $5 billion tourism industry—contributing three per cent of GDP—was devastated. The Mandarin Oriental Hostel in Jakarta saw 700 room cancellations. Again a High School soccer tournament scheduled to take place in Jakarta was moved to Malaysia. Tourism was affected adversely so much so that 12 million Indonesians felt jobless. Again foreign direct investment (FDI) came down because the investors felt hostile environment in Indonesia. They are relocating their factories in China and Vietnam. They are finding operational risks in oil and gas sectors also. Caltex Pacific Indonesia has been forced to turn over management of an oilfield in Sumatra and they are unhappy with social unrest, militant unions and rapacious local business. Many foreign companies have fled from the mining industries and new explorations have stopped.[15]

The country is facing a crisis and Al Qaida network is spreading. Driven by the ideal of a universal *Jehad*, it has been able to politicise, radicalise and mobilise Muslims. *Jemaah Islamiyah* and Moro Islamic Liberation Front (MILF) have been supported to mobilise Muslim opinion in Southeast Asia. Telephone intercepts indicated that in early 1999 at the request of *Al Qaida*'s head of external operations, Abu Zubaida, the MILF opened special camps for training foreign recruits. These camps were located in Abu Bakar complex, which was later overrun by the Philippine military.[16] Simultaneously Lashkar Jundullah established a facility in Poso in Sulawesi. JI established its cells in Singapore and Malaysia for internal subversion and the downfall of Taliban regime in Afghanistan did not alter the situation in Southeast Asia. *Al Qaida* operates in a framework that is deceptive. In addition to despatching its operatives to target countries, it provides experts, training and resources to other Islamist political and military organisations to advance a common goal. It has influenced JI, a regional organisation with overground and underground networks extending from Southern Thailand to Australia.[17] Other Southeast Asian Organisations that

*Al Qaida* has influenced are Kumpulan Mujahidin Malaysia, Laskar Jundullah Indonesia, and MILF. When JI wanted to destroy the US, British, Australian and Israeli diplomatic targets in Singapore, *Al Qaida* despatched four Afghan trained Arab suicide bombers to Southeast Asia. Striving for establishing Darulah Islamiah Raya, comprising Malaysia, Singapore, Brunei, Indonesia and Mindanao, Islamic ideologies are spreading in the Malay world against the existing order.[18]

Regarding Islamic radicals, James Hookway of Far Eastern Economic Review reported that for any new operation they attach emphasis on new converts to Islam, who are prepared to kill and die for their new found faith.[19] The phenomenon of tapping converts is strategically conceived. Initially Abu Sayyaf group in the Philippines was encouraged to engage new converts in terrorist activities, but now JI and others have picked up that methodology. Briton Richard Reid tried to blow up a US airliner flying from Paris by smuggling explosives aboard in the soles of his running shoes. In the US, Jose Padilla of Chicago tried to procure materials for constructing a radiation for a bomb. Ramzi Yousef credited to bomb World Trade Centre, had earlier come to Manila to assassinate Pope John Paul II. *Al Qaida* believes that these converts are ideal terrorists who prove more dangerous than established Muslim guerrilla groups. The new converts are often more zealous and eager to prove themselves worthy of their new faith.[20]

There is a sizeable section of population of Arab Origin, known as Hadrami, which has been supporting the rise of radical Islam in Indonesia. Their population is estimated at 5 million and they have maintained connections with the Arab World.[21] They are respected in Indonesia, because it is understood that they introduced Islam in that archipelago. They have been sending their children to study in the Arab World and therefore their knowledge of Islamic ideology and ethos are better than others. Abu Bakar Bashir is a Hadrami and his role in growing radicalisation of Islamic politics in Indonesia has been enormous. Hadrami radicals and moderates calls for the adoption of *Shariat* laws for governance of the country. Hadrami have Al Irsyad organisation which has been funding the establishment of several schools and colleges and their existence in Solo, Central Sulawesi and Maluku have attracted headlines, because some of the militants interrogated in recent years are the products of these schools and colleges. Al Irsyad operates 140 missions and several hospitals nation-wide and their positive role in the social life of the country are also significant. However problem arises because some of the Hadrami elites consider it as their duty to correct Indonesia's syncretic brand of Islam.[22] They have traditionally tended to be more conservative than their counterparts in Indonesia and indeed holier than Santri and Abangans in Java. Habib Abdul Rahman Al Habsyi, a noted Hadrami cleric, has been drawing large number of young students to classes in a mosque in Jakarta and sending hundreds to Yemen every year to study in religious schools. Airline Yemenia started twice weekly flights linking Sanaa and Jakarta directly to facilitate the movement of the people in 2002. Indonesian Muslims are taught Salafism, a school of Islam that preaches Puritanism. Alwi Shihab, a Hadrami and former foreign minister, however says that an Islamic education in Yemen should not be equated with militancy. He says that there are more fundamentalist schools in Saudi Arabia and Egypt supporting Puritanism in Islam.[23] Radical Islam is thus getting an indigenous touch and there is absence of clear consensus on how to tackle them.

Senior leaders are unable to articulate the view that extremism is a serious threat to the future of democracy and pluralism in the country and that the existence of moderate Islam are in tune with the Malay ethos. If the clerics in Solo display the sign "No prestige without *Jehad*", or if they echo the seven words of Abu Bakar, "I am a Muslim. They are infidels", or if they promote the sale of Osama T. shirt, it should be tackled at the ideological and religious levels. We are citizens of a civilised world and should not preach bloodshed deliberately against it. The founding fathers of Indonesian constitution promoted

Bhinnekka Tungul Ekka (Unity in Diversity) and unity of the nation is related with maintaining diversity of the archipelago. If *Shariat* laws are to be adopted, it is for the elected representatives to decide, and if they have to offer *Namaz* (Prayer) five times a day or observe a code of conduct, they are educated and civilised enough to decide their course of action. No sect, race or groups have any right to impose their will on fellow citizens, and thus terror groups should understand the limitations of their operations. National leaders should articulate the issues of national development and promote integrationist ideas.

Amien Rais, Chairman of the Indonesian People's Assembly, has been an influential leader for propagating moderate Islam in Indonesia. According to him, "all Muslims have to respect the invaluable existence of human beings. *Al Quran* says that when a soul happens to be pure and clean, and has never caused any earthly corruption, whoever kills the innocent soul without any reason has committed a grave crime against humanity, as if he has killed all human kind. But whoever saves a soul has done a noble act, as if he has saved the human kind".[24]

Amien Rais further stated that "here and there, now and then, there are some offensive, xenophobic statements made by Muslim teachers in the mosque. But, I can assure you that they are very small, insignificant pockets. When Taliban regime collapsed after the American attack, all people in my country were happy and excited. Why? Because to us, Taliban is a very bad advertisement for Islam. It is anti-Islamic. Islam does not prohibit a women to be educated. Islam does not order women to stay in the houses, covering all the body except the two eyes. Islam does not teach us to grow our beard whereby the beard becomes a symbol of religiosity and piety. The wonderful, noble teachings of the Prophet were reduced absurdly by the Taliban".[25]

The bloodshed in Bali has tarnished external image of Indonesia. The national moral movement—a forum of religious leaders and public figures—issued a statement on 12 November 2002 expressing their support to the government to fight against terrorism. They emphasised that no religion recommends the use of violence and the statement was signed by Hasyim Muzadi, (Chairman, Nahdlatul *Ulama*), Syafi Ma'arif (Chairman, Muhammadiyah), Cardinal Darmaatmadja (Chairman, Indonesian Bishop's Council), Roeslan Abdulgani (Freedom fighter), and Nurcholish Madjid (Muslim Intellectual). The government observed November 15 as a National day of Silence and Prayer for the Victims of Bali blast. Thousands of Balinese Hindus performed a ritual cleansing at the site of the blast and at the sea to release the souls of victims and plead for the blessings of heaven to bring spiritual and economic recovery.[26] The pictures of the victims were placed at the bomb site surrounded by incense. This was attended by ministers, ambassadors, the families of the victims and thousands of Balinese.

The national leaders by and large do not approve the actions of radical Islam advertently but they are neither vocal against them. So their silence and sophisticated opposition are considered support for the terrorist groups inadvertently. President Megawati is more careful in making statements against them because of her personal experiences. Although her party had secured the largest number of seats in the DPR, she could not be elected the President in 1999 on the basis of her genealogy. It is known that she had a Hindu mother and if she becomes aggressive against radical Muslims in her country, she will be projected anti-Muslim once again. It will be very difficult for her to come back to power. But as a Javanese, she is determined to fight against terrorism slowly and effectively. She is in search of a new vision and strategy for reforms and this will take care of various problems in the country.

Although *Al Qaida* and JI have their foothold and their followers claim allegiance of many, it is a established fact that moderates are in majority. Indonesia for centuries have been influenced by world's major religious systems, namely Hinduism, Buddhism, Islam, Christianity and Confucianism. Indonesian Islam has engaged with other faiths, adapting and adopting the cultural traditions of diverse people.[27] Islamic expression is very different in Indonesia compared to puritanical brand that has been nurtured in the Arab world. It has been moderate, tolerant and progressive for centuries. Karim Raslan has explained that this modernisation is because of geography and history. Being closer to Indian subcontinent geographically and located en route Lombok, Malacca and Sunda Straits—it tended to remain syncretic. Historically, Islam's spread in Indonesia was through peaceful means, by Arab and Indian traders and preachers. It spread peacefully and there was no Jehad for conversions. Indonesia emerged as a unique centre of Islam when one could find the amalgam of the essence of major religions of the world. Indonesian Islam also contributed new chapters in the existing philosophy of Islam, the concept of ijtihad—the spirit of questioning, self criticism and renewal—that placed Islam at the vanguard of science, technology and civil society.[28] Ijtihad is ignored in the Arab world but it is an important subject of understanding in Indonesia. Santri and Abangans are devout and conversant with the *Koran*, familiar with classical Islamic works and trained in fiqh (Islamic jurisprudence). They have the confidence to debate and confront their own ultra-conservative co-religionists on anything from Jehad to women's rights.[29] These Muslims are humble and compassionate and they know what is decent and what is rubbish and brutish.

To conclude, it may be observed that although the number of Islamic radicals have increased and terror groups activated, the moderate elements have potentials to promote resilience, pluralism and democracy. They know their history and realities of social life. They draw inspirations from the heroes of the Srivijayan, Majapahit and colonial periods. Though they went to battlegrounds intermittently in the past, it was never for forcible conversions. There had been widespread bloodshed in Indonesia during 1965-69 to contain communism, but it was motivated politically. Some observers projected this phenomenon as *Jehad* but this had nothing to do with the spread of Islamic religion.

Anti-communist crusades simply strengthened the foundations of military rule under the stewardship of General Suharto. This *Jehad* simply proved retrogressive, the manifestations of which became transparent in due course. Indonesia does not need bloodshed but peace, resilience and good governance to establish themselves as a secular model amongst the Islamic world. It has to reflect the essence of Malay culture in order to remain united and strong.

## References


1. Press statement issued in Jakarta, 13 October 2002.
2. The Times of India, 14 October 2002.
3. *Ibid.*, 17 October 2002.
4. *Ibid.*, 18 October 2002.
5. *Ibid.*, 22 October 2002.
6. Ulil Abshar - Abdalla, "Silent Witness,", Time, 28 October 2002, p.45.
7. Andrew Marshal, "The Rage Culture", Time, 28 October 2002, pp52-57.
8. Antara in News from Indonesia, Embassy of the Republic of Indonesia, New Delhi, no.24, December 2001, p.5
9. The Jakarta Post in News from Indonesia, January 2002, p.5.
10. The Jakarta Post in News from Indonesia, no.9, September 2002, p.3.
11. The Jakarta Post, 3 October 2002 and 7 October 2002.
12. *Ibid.*
13. Yusril Ihza Mahendra, "Shared Responsibility in Combating Terrorism: Post-Bali Tragedy", News from Indonesia, November 2002, no.11, pp.26-27.
14. Michael Schuman, "A Failed State", Time, 28 October 2002, p.46.
15. *Ibid.*, pp.46-50.
16. Rohan Gunaratna, "Al Qaida in the Asia-Pacific", IIAS Newsletter, Leiden, 14 June 2002, p.4.
17. *Ibid.*
18. *Ibid.*
19. James Hookway, 'How a Terrorist Proves his faith", Far Eastern Economic Review, 14 November 2002, pp14-15.
20. *Ibid.*
21. Dini Djalal, "Where Terror is Taught", *Ibid.*, p.18.
22. *Ibid.*
23. *Ibid.*, p.19.

24. Amien Rais, "The War Against Terrorism in Indonesia", IIAS Newsletter, No.28, 20 March 2002, p.1
25. *Ibid.*, p.3
26. The Jakarta Post, 16 November 2002
27. Karim Raslan, "The Moderate Majority", Time, 28 October 2002, p.57
28. *Ibid.*
29. *Ibid.*

# 7

# Conclusion

Indonesia is facing a transitional phase from dictatorship to democracy when institutional faith in the government of the people, for the people and by the people, is yet to percolate down in the political system. The threat of the military rule has not been dissipated as the social unrest and economic deterioration continues. No country in the region would like to see Indonesia embroiled in the crises for too long, because their stability and boom is linked with Indonesia, the largest state in the ASEAN. The ASEAN countries, whether civilian or military, can support any group, if they are able to put Indonesia on the development track. However, it is difficult to find a ready-made solution for the gigantic problems of Indonesia, which has been complicated in recent years.

There are two issues, which apparently, are major threats for the evolving political system. Firstly, there is the threat of fundamentalism. *Darul* Islam and *Masjumi* followers are demanding the declaration of Islamic state. They are opposing Panchasila as the state philosophy, and believe that the adherents of other religions are infidels. They are strongly preaching the ethics of holywar (*Jehad*) and are involved in organised crime in Aceh, Irian Jaya and Ambon. Their roles in communal riots have generated ethnic tension in all parts of the country.

Secondly, the separatist movement has shaken the foundation of the Indonesian republic. There is intense struggle for autonomy or independence in Aceh, Ambon and Irian Jaya. There have been disturbances in West Timor (*Nusa Tenggara*) after the separation of East Timor as an independent state. Besides these areas, we have found incidents of rioting and violence in other parts of the country as well. In fact, there are hundreds of ethnic groups and all of them would like to preserve their separate identity. Sukarno, the father of the nation, nurtured and cared for all the ethnic groups, in order to promote common nationalism. But when he was ousted from power, anti-Sukarno campaign was launched to tarnish his image and contributions. Suharto, his successor, remained in power with the support of the armed forces. He was authoritarian and suppressed the opposition for 32 years. It was difficult to diagnose the simmering dissent, which exploded massively in 1998. The unrest continues and the prevailing situation can come under control only by dialogue, persuasion and progress.

A glimpse of the ethnic disputes shows that the situation is disturbing. Timorese for example, are of Melanesian stock, whose claim for territoriality is spread over both parts, but one of them is an integral part of Indonesia and the other has become independent. There has been massive exodus of population from East Timor of Javanese and Bugis, numbering about 50,000, who transmigrated in that area after 1976. It is understood that 100,000 Timorese had been massacred in 1975 and similarly thousands were killed in 1999 when the referendum for independence took place. An overwhelming majority of the people are Christians and Islam never went on this island. Most of the indigenous people are dark skinned and light built and there are 36 distinct ethnic linguistic groups. However there is no link between Bahasa Indonesia and the languages of the Timorese. Some of the Melanesians still believe in animism. The farmer still spills blood before tilling the soil and according to their traditional system, they worship crocodile (the fertility god), and the figure of a crocodile is used in Timorese weaving motifs. Their integration into the national mainstream is difficult indeed, particularly after the separation of East Timor as an independent state. The exodus from East Timor to West Timor and now from West Timor to other provinces has posed serious threat to national integration.

Another ethnic group, which has posed a challenge to the country is the ethnic Chinese, numbering about 6.5 million population. The Chinese are comparatively well off and they have excelled as businessmen, bankers, professionals, traders, shopkeepers, mechanics, tour-guides, plantation owners and overseers in Indonesia and have generated jealousy of the native population. They control the economy and they are targeted as the main enemy of the economic crisis. There have been anti-Chinese riots since 1998. Their shops have been looted, women have been raped and properties damaged. More than 70,000 people left Indonesia in 1998 who felt insecure in the country. Hence, the pertinent question is whether Indonesia will survive economically without the Chinese entrepreneurs and their capital?

Another thorn in the path of national integration is Aceh, where there is call to massacre government troops stationed there. Aceh Merdeka under Mustafa Abubakar, believes in religious extremism. As Aceh was one of the first part of the archipelago to be converted to Islam, it is the bedrock of Islamic religion and culture. Numbering about three million people, they are highly Islamic. Most of them read and write Arabic and pray in Arabic. Their language, Acehnese, have lot of words from the Cham language and they are different from Bahasa Indonesia. They have been demanding autonomy or independence and in order to press their demands have formed Free Aceh Movement, which believes in guerrilla warfare. Indonesian troops have tried to terrorise the people and indulged in massacres, and some mass graves have been found in the recent past, but that has not subdued the people. Acehnese have become very active after the separation of East Timor, and forced President Abudurrahman Wahid to announce referendum on the pattern of East Timor, but subsequently he had to withdraw the offer on one pretext or the other.

Yet another ethnic group, which draws our attention are the *Ambonese* in Maluku province. The Ambonese, also called "black Dutch", were the Dutch minded people, who had been trained by the Dutch colonial masters to fight Indonesian revolutionaries in the post 1945 era. The Ambonese are generally people of mixed race of Portuguese, Alfuros, Malays, Javanese and Dutch decent. The mixed blood is most obvious in the lighter-skinned coastal villages. The people in the countryside have darker complexion and more pronounced Melanesian features. Ambonese speak a dialect belonging to Melayo-Polynesian groups. Religion-wise most of them are Protestants. It has been the famous spice-island, where there is an excellent harbour. They are also interested in establishing a Republic Maluku Selatan and have been critical of the central government. There was a serious riot in January 1999 between Christians and the Muslim population in Ambon. The riots started after three mosques and three churches were torched on the occasion of *Idul-Fitr*. Over 88 (eighty-eight) homes were burnt and many cars were set on fire. Guardian (London), reported that 24 Christians were massacred in the Church by the Muslim mobs on 12 August 1999 and equally some Muslims were also killed. A spokesman for Ambon*'s* Al-Fatah mosque confirmed that at least 60 Muslims were killed and 50 others were wounded. The situation has become so serious that there has been exodus of thirty thousand people from Ambon to other areas and the communal life remains disturbed. Radical Muslims are preaching that there should be *Jehad* to take revenge and the conflict remains unresolved.

Lastly, we have to examine the problems in Irian Jaya where the separatist movement is strong. The indigenous people of that island are mainly Melanesians and their integration into the national mainstream is still a distant dream. Their voice is articulated by the Free Papua Movement (OPM) since 1960 and they have been waging a low level guerrilla-war. Situated on the border of Papua New Guinea and far away from Jakarta, this area has been very sensitive.

Needless to say, the principle of unity in diversity (Bhinneka Tunggul Ika) needs infusion of new spirit to make inter-ethnic and inter-communal life harmonious. The spirit of tolerance and accommodation needs to be enforced and growth of all sorts of fundamentalist ideas curbed. There is a need to spread the gospel of "live and let live". No community should be given an impression that "big fish will eat smaller ones". Indonesia is very rich in natural resources. It has gold mines and great reservoir of oil. It has also got timber, rubber, coffee, sugar, copper besides a huge manpower. For its prosperity, it simply needs a good governance, political stability and efficient economic management. As it is mosaic of different cultures and ethnic groups, Indonesia is naturally endowed to articulate the voice of Asia at the global level.

As far as the constitution of the country is concerned, three constitutions have been framed. The first in 1945, second in 1949 and the third in 1950. The constitution of 1945 is enforced, but there have been no amendments for decades. There has been lot of transformations in the country at the social and political level, and several amendments are needed to cope with the challenges facing the country. Again, care is needed to balance division of powers so that the omissions and commissions of the Presidency might be checked.

Islam has to be given due importance in the polity because that is the religion of the overwhelming majority, but other religions cannot be bulldozed. They have tolerated Hinduism and Christianity for long and they have evolved a distinct Indonesian culture. Hindus are in majority in Bali and the Christians are in majority in Ambon and Kupang. Their social and religious organisations are formidable and there is a need to evolve a system in which they feel secure and prosperous. As the low profile of Indonesia helped ASEAN to grow, similarly the low profile of the Javanese can help the trends towards national integration.

To sum up, Indonesia needs a federation in which major islands should be authorised to take decisions for rule making, rule application and rule adjudication. As Indonesia is large and heterogeneous, its problems too are large and heterogeneous and they differ from one place to another. If the powers are decentralised and strong monitoring system is evolved, the results might be desirable. Finally it can be stated that Indonesian society and politics display striking similarities with India and both need to learn from the experiences of one another.

# Appendix

## The 1945 Constitution of the Republic of the Indonesia

The Opening to the Constitution

The 1945 Constitution

Transitional Provisions

Elucidation of the Constitution

The System of Government of the State

Decree of 5th July 1959

### The Opening to the Constitution

Whereas Independence is the natural right of every nation, colonialism must be abolished in this world because it is not in conformity with humanity and Justice.

And the struggle of the movement for the independence of Indonesia has now reached the hour of rejoicing by leading the People of Indonesia safe and sound to the gateway of the Independence of an Indonesian State which is free, united, sovereign, just and prosperous.

Thanks to the blessing of God Almighty and impelled by the noble desire to lead their own free national life, the People of Indonesia hereby declare their independence.

Following this, in order to set up a government of the State of Indonesia which shall protect the whole of the Indonesian People and their entire native land of Indonesia, and in order to advance the general welfare, to develop the intellectual life of the nation and to contribute in implementing an order in the world which is based upon independence, abiding peace and social justice, the structure of Indonesia's National Independence shall be formulated in a Constitution of the Indonesian State which shall have the structural state form of a Republic of Indonesia with sovereignty of the People, and which shall be based upon : Belief in the One, Supreme God, just and civilised Humanity, the unity of Indonesia, and democracy which guided by the inner wisdom in the unanimity arising out of deliberation amongst representatives, meanwhile creating a condition of social justice for the whole of the People of Indonesia.

## The Constitution

### Chapter I. Form and Sovereignty

*Article 1*

1. The State of Indonesia shall be a unitary state which has the form of a Republic.
2. Sovereignty shall be in the hands of the People and shall be exercised in full by the Majelis Permusyawaratan Rakyat.

### Chapter II. The Majelis Permusyawaratan Rakyat

*Article 2.*

1. The Majelis Permusyawaratan Rakyat shall consist of members of the Dewan Perwakilan Rakyat augmented by delegates from the regional territories and the groups in accordance with regulations prescribed by statute.sit at least once in every five years in the capital of the State.
2. The Majelis Permusyawaratan Rakyat shall sit at least once in every five years in the capital of the State.
3. All decisions of the Majelis Permusyawaratan Rakyat shall be determined by majority vote.

*Article 3.*

The Majelis Permusyawaratan Rakyat shall determine the Constitution and the broad lines of the policy of the State.

## Chapter III. The Powers of Government of the State

*Article 4.*

1. The President of the Republic of Indonesia shall hold the power of government in accordance with the Constitution.
2. In exercising his duties, the President shall be assisted by a Vice-President.

*Article 5.*

1. The President shall hold the power to make statutes in agreement with the Dewan Perwakilan Rakyat.
2. The President shall determine the government Regulations necessary to implement statutes.

*Article 6.*

1. The President shall be a native-born Indonesian.
2. The President and Vice-President shall be elected by the Majelis Permusyawaratan Rakyat by majority vote.

*Article 7.*

The President and Vice-President shall hold office for a term of five years and shall be eligible for re-election.

*Article 8.*

Should the President die, cease from executing or be unable to execute his duties during his term of office, his office shall be taken by the Vice-President until the expiry of that term.

*Article 9.*

Before assuming the duties of office, the President and Vice-President shall take an oath according to the requirements of religion, or shall make a solemn promise, before the Majelis Permusyawaratan Rakyat or the Dewan Perwakilan Rakyat, as follows:

Oath of the President (Vice-President)

"I swear before God that, to the best of my ability, I will fulfill as justly as possible the duties of the President (Vice-President) of the Republic of Indonesia; that I will hold faithfully to the Constitution and conscientiously implement all statutes and regulations, and that I will devote myself to the service of Country and Nation".

Promise of the President (Vice-President)

"I solemnly promise that, to the best of my ability, I will fulfill as justly as possible the duties of the President (Vice-President) of the Republic of Indonesia; that I will hold faithfully to the Constitution and conscientiously implement all statutes and regulations, and that I will devote myself to the service of Country and Nation".

*Article 10.*

The President shall hold the highest authority over the Army, the Navy and Air Force.

*Article 11.*

The President, with the agreement of the Dewak Prewakilan Rakyat, declares war, makes peace and concludes treaties with other states.

*Article 12.*

The President declares the state of emergency. The conditions governing, and the consequences of, the state of emergency shall be prescribed by statute.

*Article 13.*

1. The President appoints diplomatic representatives and consuls.
2. The President receives the diplomatic representatives of other states.

*Article 14.*

The President grants grace, amnesties, abolitions and restoration of rights.

*Article 15.*

The President grants titles, decorations and other marks of honour.

**Chapter IV. The Supreme Advisory Council**

*Article 16.*

1. The structure of the Supreme Advisory Council shall be prescribed by statute.
2. This council shall submit replies to issues raised by the President and shall have the right to submit proposals to the Government.

**Chapter V. The Ministers of the State**

*Article 17.*

1. The President shall be assisted by ministers of the State.
2. These Ministers shall be appointed and dismissed by the President.
3. These Ministers shall lead the Government Departments.

**Chapter VI. Local Government**

*Article 18*

The division of the area of Indonesia into large and small regional territories together with the structures of their administrations, shall be prescribed by statute, with regard for and in observance of the principle of deliberation in the governmental system of the State, and the traditional rights in the regional territories which have a special character.

**Chapter VII. The Dewan Perwakilan Rakyat (The Legislative Body)**

*Article 19.*

1. (1) The structure of the Dewan Perwakilan Rakyat shall be prescribed by statute.
2. (2) The Dewan Perwakilan Rakyat shall sit at least once a year.

*Article 20.*

1. (1) Every statute shall require the agreement of the Dewan Perwakilan Rakyat.
2. (2) Should a draft law not obtain the agreement of the Dewan Perwakilan Rakyat, that draft may not be submitted again during the same session of the Dewan Perwakilan Rakyat.

*Article 21.*

1. Members of the Dewan Perwakilan Rakyat shall have the right to submit draft laws.
2. Should those drafts, although agreed to by the Dewan Perwakilan Rakyat, not be ratified by the President, those drafts may not be submitted again during the same session of the Dewan Perwakilan Rakyat.

*Article 22*

1. Should exigency compel, the President shall have the right to determine Government Regulations in lieu of statutes.
2. Those Government Regulations must obtain the agreement of the Dewan Perwakilan Rakyat in its next session.

Should that agreement not be obtained, the Government Regulation shall be revoked.

## Chapter VII. Finance

*Article 23.*

1. The estimates of revenue and expenditure shall be fixed each year by statute. Should the Dewan Perwakilan Rakyat not agree to the estimates proposed by the Government, the Government shall work to the estimates of the previous year.
2. All kinds of taxes for the needs of the State shall be based upon statutes.
3. All kinds of values of the currency shall be prescribed by statute.

4. Further matters of the finances of the state shall be regulated by statute.
5. In order to investigate the accountability for state Finances, a Body for the investigation of finance shall be set up, the regulations for which shall be set up, the regulations for which shall be prescribed by statute.

The results of that investigation shall be made known to the Dewan Perwakilan Rakyat.

**Chapter IX. The Judicial Powers**

*Article 24.*

1. The Judicial powers shall be exercised by a Supreme Court and other courts of law in accordance with statute.
2. The structure and powers of those courts of law shall be regulated by statute.

*Article 25.*

The conditions for becoming a judge and for being dismissed shall be prescribed by statute.

**Chapter X. Citizens**

*Article 26.*

1. Citizens shall be persons who are native-born Indonesians and persons of other nationality who are legalised by statue as being citizens.
2. Conditions with regard to citizenship shall be prescribed by statute.

*Article 27.*

1. Without any exception, all citizens shall have equal position in Law and Government and shall be obliged to uphold that Law and Government.
2. Every citizen shall have the right to work, and to a living, befitting for human beings.

*Article 28.*

Freedom of association and assembly, of expressing thoughts and of issuing writing and the like, shall be prescribe by statute.

## Chapter XI. Religion

*Article 29.*

1. The State shall be based upon Belief in the One, Supreme God.
2. The State shall guarantee freedom to every resident to adhere to his respective religion and to perform his religious duties in conformity with that religion and that faith.

## Chapter XII. Defence

*Article 30.*

1. Every citizen shall have the right and the duty to participate in the defence effort of the State.
2. Conditions Concerning defence shall be regulated by statute.

## Chapter XII. Education

*Article 31.*

1. Every citizen shall have the right to obtain an education.
2. The Government shall establish and contract a national educational system which shall be regulated by statute.

*Article 32.*

The Government shall advance the national culture of Indonesia.

## Chapter XIV: Social well-being

*Article 33.*

1. The economy shall be organised as a common endeavour based upon the principle of the family system.
2. Branches of production which are important for the State and which affect the life of most people shall be controlled by the State.

3. Land and water and the natural riches contained therein shall be controlled by the State and shall be made use of for the people.

*Article 34.*

The poor and destitute children, shall be cared for by the State.

**Chapter XV. Flag and Language**

*Article 35*

The Flag of the Indonesian State shall be the Honoured Red and White.

*Article 36.*

The Language of the State shall be the Indonesian Language.

**Chapter XVI. Alternations to the Constitution**

*Article 37.*

1. In order to alter the Constitution, at least two-thirds of the total members of the Majelis Permusyawaratan Rakyat must be in attendance.
2. A decision shall be taken with the agreement of at least two-thirds of the total number of members who are in attendance.

## 3. Transitional Provisions

**Clause I**

The Preparatory Committee for Indonesia's Independence shall regulate and execute the transfer of government to the Indonesian Government.

**Clause II**

All existing institutions and regulations of the State shall continue to function so long as new ones have not been set up in conformity with this Constitution.

**Clause III**

The President and Vice-President shall be elected for the first time by the Preparatory Committee for Indonesia's Independence.

**Clause IV**

Before the Majelis Permusyawaratan Rakyat the Dewan Perwakilan Rakyat and the Supreme Advisory Council have been set up in conformity with this Constitution, all their powers shall be exercised by the President with the assistance of a National Committee.

**Additional Provisions**

3. Within six months after the end of the Greater East Asia War, The President of Indonesia shall regulate and implement all things which are stipulated in this Constitution.
4. Within six months after the Majelis Permusyawaratan Rakyat has bee set up, the Majelis shall sit in order to determine the Constitution.

## 4. Elucidation of the Constitution (General)

### 1. The written Constitution, a part of Fundamental Law

The written Constitution of a state is only a part of the Law which is the basis o that State. The Constitution is that part of the Fundamental Law which is written down, while beside that Constitution there also prevails Fundamental Law which is not written down, namely, the basic rules which arise and are maintained in the practice of running a state, although they are not written down.

Certainly, in order to study the Fundamental Law (Droit Constitutional) of a state, it is not enough only to study the articles of its written Constitution (Loi Constitutionnel) alone, but one must also study how it is applied and what is the spiritual background (geistlichen Hinterground, of that written Constitution.

The Constitution of any state whatsoever can not be understood if merely its text is read alone. Truly, to understand the meaning of the Constitution of a state, we must also study how that text came into being, we must know the explanations made of it and we must also know under what conditions that text was made.

In this way we shall be able to understand what is the meaning and purpose of the Constitution we are studying and what current of thought it was which became the foundation of that Constitution.

**2. Fundamental ideals in the "Opening" (Preamble)**

What are the fundamentals contained in the Preamble to the Constitution?

1. The State—so the next runs—is what 'shall protect the whole of the Indonesian People and their entire native land of Indonesia—based upon... unity—meanwhile creating a condition of social justice for the whole of the People of Indonesia".
2. In this Preamble, the current of thought is accepted of the unitary state, the state which protects and covers the whole of the people. Thus the state encompasses every kind of group opinion, encompasses all opinions of individuals. The state, in accordance with concept of this Preamble, seeks unity, and extends over the whole of the Indonesian People. This is one foundation of the state which may not be forgotten.
3. The third fundamental contained in the Preamble is that of sovereignty of the people, based upon democracy and deliberation amongst representatives. Therefore, the system of state which is given form in the Constitution must be based upon sovereignty of the people and must be based upon deliberation amongst representatives. Indeed, this current of thought accords with the character of Indonesian society.

4. The fourth fundamental idea contained in the Preamble is that the state is based upon that Belief in the One, Supreme God which conforms with the principles of just and civilised humanity.

Therefore, the Constitution must oblige the Government and other authorities o the state to nurture the nobility of human character and to hold fast to the fine moral ideals of the people.

## III. The Constitution gives form in its articles to the Fundamental Ideas contained in the Preamble

The above fundamental ideas pervade the spiritual background of the Constitution of the State of Indonesia. These fundamental ideas give rise to those ideals of law (Rechtsidee) which dominate the Fundamental Law of the State, both written law (the Constitution) and unwritten law.

The Constitution gives form to these fundamental ideas in its articles.

## IV. The Constitution is Short and Flexible in Character

The Constitution has only 37 articles. The other paragraphs contain only additional and transitional provisions. This draft is thus very brief when compared, for instance, with the Constitution o the Philippines.

It is enough if the Constitution contains only fundamental rules, contains only broad lines of instruction to the Central Government and to other authorities of the State for conducting the life of the State and providing social well-being. Especially for a new state and a young state, it is better if that written Fundamental Law contains only basic rules, whilst the provisions implementing those basic rules are left statutes which are more easily draw up, altered and revoked.

This is the system of the Constitution.

We must always remember the dynamic of the life of Indonesian society and state Indonesian society and state are growing, the era is changing, especially during this present period of physical and spiritual revolution.

Therefore, we must live dynamically, we must watch every kind of movement in the life of Indonesian society and state. In that connection, let us not precipitately crystallise, provide form to (Gestaltung), ideas which can still easily alter.

Certainly it is the nature of those written rules to be binding. For that reason, the more flexible ("elastic") those rules are, the better. Thus we must guard against the Constitutional system being left behind the times. Let us not go so far as to make a constitution which is quickly out-moded (verouderd). What is extremely important in the administration and in the life of the state is the spirit, the spirit of the authorities of the state, the spirit of the leaders of the administration. Although a constitution is drawn up which, according to the letter, is characterised by the family principle, in the spirit of the authorities of the state, the leaders of the administration, be individualistic, that Constitution is certain to have no meaning is not perfect, if the spirit of the authorities of the administration is good, that constitution will certainly not obstruct the course o the state. Thus what is most important is the spirit. That spirit is a living thing, or, in other words, it is dynamic. In connection with this, only the fundamental rules alone must be laid down in the constitution, whilst what is necessary for executing those fundamental rules must be left to statutes.

## The System of Government of the State

The system of the government of the State which is stipulated in the Constitution is:

*Indonesia is a State Based on Law "Rechtstaat"*

1. The state of Indonesia is based upon Law (Rechtstaat), it is not based upon mere power (Machtstaat)

*The System is Constitutional*

2. The government is based upon Constitutionalism (Fundamental Law), not absolutism (authority without limits)

*The Highest Authority of the State is in the Hands of the Majelis Permusyawaratan Rakyat ("die gesamte Staatsgewalt liegt allein bei der Majelis").*

3. The sovereignty of the people is held by a body named the Majelis Permusyawaratan Rakyat as the embodiment of the whole of the People of Indonesia (Vertretungsorgan des Willens des Staatvolkes). This Majelis determines the Constitution and determines the broad lines of the policy of the state. The Majelis appoints the Head of State (President) and the Vice Head of State (Vice-President).

It is this Majelis which holds the highest authority of the State, whilst the President must execute the policy of the State according tot he broad lines which have been determined by the Majelis.

The President, who is appointed by the Majelis, is subordinate to and responsible to the Majelis. He is the "mandatory" of the Majelis, he is obliged to execute the decisions of the Majelis.

The President is not "neben" but is "untergeordnet" to the Majelis.

*The President is the Highest Executive of the Government of the State below the Majelis.*

Below the Majelis Permusyawaratan Rakyat, the President is the Highest Executive of the Government of the State.

In conducting the administration of the State, authority and responsibility are in the hands of the President (concentration of power and responsibility upon the President),

*The President is Not Responsible to the dewan Perwakilan Rakyat.*

Beside the President there is the Dewan Perwakilan Rakyat. The President must obtain the agreement of the Dewan Perwakilan Rakyat in order to make laws (gesetz gebung) and in order to fix the estimates of the revenues and expenditures of the State (Staatsbegroting).

Because of this, the President must work together with the Dewan Perwakilan Rakyat, but the President is not responsible to the dewan, which means that the Presidents position is not dependent upon the Dewan.

*The Ministers of the State are Assistants to the President : The Ministers of the state are Not responsible to the dewan Perwakilan Rakyat.*

The President appoints and dismisses the Ministers of the State. Those Ministers are not responsible to the Dewan Perwakilan Rakyat. Their positions are not dependent upon the Dewan but are dependent upon the President. They are the assistants of the President.

*The Authority of the Head of State is Not Unlimited*

Although the Head of State is not responsible to the Dewan Perwakilan Rakyat, he is not a "dictator", which means that his authority is not unlimited.

It has been stressed above that he is responsible to the Majelis Permusyawaratan Rakyat. Apart from this, he must carefully and thoroughly pay attention to the voice of the Dewan Perwakilan Rakyat.

*The Position of the Dewan Perwakilan Rakyat.*

The position of the dewak Perwakilan Rakyat is strong. The Dewan can not be dissolved by the President. (This is at variance with the parliamentary system.) Apart from this, the members of the Dewan are all of them concurrently members of the Majelis Permusyawaratan Rakyat. For that reason the Dewan Perwakilan Rakyat can at all times control the acts of the President, and if the dewan considers that the President has in fact transgressed against the policy of the state determined by the Constitution or by the Majelis Permusyawaratan Rakyat, the Majelis can be called for a special siting so that it can ask the President to account for his responsibility.

The Ministers of the State are Not Ordinary High Ranking Civil Servants.

Although the positions of the Ministers of the State are dependent upon the President, nevertheless they are not ordinary high-ranking civil servants, because it is those Ministers who, in the first place, in practice execute the authority of the Government (pouvoir execitif).

As the leaders of Departments, the Ministers know the ins and outs of matters connected with their jurisdictions. In connection with this, the Ministers have great influence upon the President in determining that part of the state's policy with which their Departments are concerned. Indeed, what is intended is that the Ministers are Leaders of the state.

In determining Government policy and in co-ordinating the administration of the State, the Ministers work together as closely as possible, one with the other, under the leadership of the President.

## Concerning the Articles

### Chapter I. The Form and Sovereignty of the State

*Article 1.*

This prescribes that the form of the state shall be unitary and a Republic, and contains the fundamental idea of sovereignty of the People.

The Majelis Permusyawaratan Rakyat is the highest organ of the state. This Majelis is considered to be the embodiment of the People which holds the sovereignty of the State.

**Chapter II. The Majelis Permusyawaratan Rakyat**

*Article 2.*

*Clause I.*

The intention is that the whole of the people, all the groups and all the regional territories throughout the country, shall have representatives in the Majelis, so that the Majelis can truly be considered to be the embodiment of the People.

What are referred to as "groups" are Bodies such as co-operatives, workers associations and other collective bodies. A rule such as this is indeed in harmony with the trend of the times. In connection with the recommendation to establish the co-operative system in the economy, this clause recalls the existence of groups in economic organisations.

*Clause 2.*

This organ which will have a large total membership, sits at least once in five years. At least once, therefore if necessary of course it may sit more than once in five years by holding special sessions.

*Article 3.*

Because the Majelis Permusyawaratan Rakyat holds the sovereignty of the State, its powers are not limited: in view of the dynamic of society, once in five years the Majelis reviews everything which has happened and considers all the trends at that time, and determines what policies it desires tobe used for the future.

**Chapter III. The Powers of Government of the State**

*Article 4 and Article 5, Clause 2.*

The President is the head of the executive power in the State. In order to execute laws, he possesses the power to prescribe government regulations (pouvoir reglementair).

*Article 5, clause 1.*

Apart from the executive power, the President together with the Dewan Perwakilan Rakyat exercises the legislative power in the state.

*Article 6, 7, 8, 9.*

Already clear.

Articles 10, 11, 12, 13, 14, 15.

The powers of the President provided by these articles are consequences of the President's position as Head of State.

## Chapter IV. The Supreme Advisory Council

*Article 16.*

This Council is a Council of State which is obliged to provide considered views to the Government. It is purely an advisory body.

## Chapter V. The Ministers of the State

*Article 17.*

See above

## Chapter VI. Local Government

*Article 18.*

1. Because the State of Indonesia is a unitary state, Indonesia, therefore, will not have within its jurisdiction areas which have the character of "states".

The area of Indonesia will be divided into provinces and these provinces will likewise be divided into smaller regional territories. These regional territories will have an utonomous character (streek-and locale rechtsge-meenschappen), titles of so called autonomous areas during the colonial period, or have the character of purely administrative regions, all tobe in accord with rules tobe laid down by statute.

In those regional territories with an autonomous character, local representative bodies will be set up, because local government also will be founded upon the principle of deliberation.

2. Within the territory of the State of Indonesia there are to be found about 250 Zelfbesturende landschappen, and Volksgemeenschappen, titles of so called self-governing localities during the colonial period, such as the desa of Java and Bali, the nagri of minangkabau, the dusun and marga: names of various social-administrative units.

Those localities have their own traditional structures, and for this reason can be considered to have a special character.

The State of the Republic of Indonesia respects the position of the said special regional territories, and all its regulations affecting those areas will bear in mind their traditional rights.

**Chapter VII. The Dewan Perwakilan Rakyat**

*Articles 19, 20, 21 and 23.*

See above.

The Dewan Perwakilan Rakyat must give its agreement to each and every draft law originating with the Government. The Dewan Perwakilan Rakyat also possesses the right to initiate legislation.

3. The Dewan also possesses the hk begroting (right to fix the budget article 23). Through this right, the Dewan controls the Government.

It must also be recalled that all members of the dewan Perwakilan Rakyat are concurrently members of the Majelis Permusyawaratan Rakyat.

*Article 22.*

This article concerns the noodverordeningsrecht (right to make emergency regulations) of the President. Such a provision is indeed necessary, so that the safety of the State can be ensured by the Government in critical conditions which compel the

Government to take quick and appropriate action. Although this is so, the Government is not, however, to be released from the control of the Dewan Perwakilan Rakyat. Therefore, the Government Regulations referred to in this article, which have the same force as laws, have also to be ratified by the dewan Perwakilan Rakyat.

**Chapter VIII Finance**

*Article 23, clauses 1, 2, 3, 4,*

Clause I lays down the budget-making right of the Dewan Perwakilan Rakyat.

The method of fixing the estimates of revenues and expenditures is a criterion of the character of the government of a state. In countries based upon fascism, those estimates are fixed solely by the administration. But in democratic states or states based upon sovereignty of the people, such as the Republic of Indonesia, the estimates of revenues and expenditures are fixed by statute, which means: with the agreement of the dewan Perwakilan Rakyat.

How the People—as a nation—shall live, and from where the expenses for living shall be obtained must be determined the People themselves through the intermediary of their representative body. The People determine their own fate and therefore their way or life also,

Article 23 states that in fixing revenues and expenditures, the position of the Dewan Perwakilan Rakyat is stronger than the position of the Government. This is a sign of the sovereignty of the People.

Because the fixing of expenditures concerns the right of the People to determine their own fate, all measures placing burdens upon the people, such as taxes etc. must be prescribed by state, that is, with the agreement of the dewan Perwakilan Rakyat.

Also the kinds and values of currency are prescribed by state. This is important because the position of the currency has great influence upon the community. Money in the first place is an instrument of exchange and of measurement of value. As an instrument of exchange its purpose is to facilitate exchange—buying and selling—in society. It follows from this that is necessary that there be those kinds and forms of money needed by the people as measures of value as a basis for fixing the worth of the respective goods which are exchanged. The thing which becomes the measure of value must have fixed worth, it must not be allowed to rise and fall because of the unregulated condition of the money. Therefore, the state of the currency must be prescribed by statute.

Related to this, the position of Bank Indonesia, which is to issue and to regulate the circulation of paper money, is prescribed by statute.

*Clause 5.*

The way in which the Government makes use of the allocations already agreed by the dewan Perwakilan Rakyat must be in keeping with that decision. In order to investigate the Government's responsibilities in this respect, a body is needed which is free from the Government's influence and authority. A body which is subordinate to the Government could not perform so heavy a duty. On the other hand, neither is that body one which stands above the Government.

Because of this, the powers and duties of that body are prescribed by statute.

## Chapter IX: The Judicial Powers

The judicial powers are powers which are independent, which means that they are free from the influence of the government's authority. Therefore, Guarantees must be established by statute concerning the position of judges.

**Chapter X. Citizens**

*Article 26, clause I.*

People of other nations, for instance, people of Dutch descent, of Chinese descent and of Arab descent, whoa re domiciled in Indonesia, who recognise Indonesia as their country and who are loyal to the State of the Republic of Indonesia, can become citizens.

*Article 26, clause 2.*

Already clear.

*Articles 27, 30 and 31 clause 1.*

These articles concern the rights of citizens.

*Articles 28, 29 clause 1 and 34.*

These articles concern the position of the residents.

The articles referred to here, both those which concern citizens alone as well as those which concern all residents, contain the desire of the Indonesian people to build a state with a democratic character which seeks to put into practice social justice and the principle of humanity.

**Chapter XI. Religion**

*Article 29, Clause 1.*

This clause states the belief of the Indonesian people in the One, Supreme God.

**Chapter XII. Defence of the State**

*Article 30,*

Already Clear.

## Chapter XIII. Education

*Article 31, clause 2.*

The nation's culture is that culture which grows as the outcome of the endeavours expressing the personality and vitality of the entire People of Indonesia.

The ancient and indigenous cultures which are to be found as cultural heights in all the regions throughout Indonesia are part of the nation's culture. Cultural efforts should lead towards advances in civilisation, culture and unity without rejecting from foreign cultures new materials which can bring about the development of or enrich the nation's own culture, as well as to raise the height of humanity of the Indonesian nation.

## Chapter XIV. Social well-being

*Article 33.*

In Article 33 there is laid down the basis of economic democracy, production by all for all, under the leadership or control of the members of society. It is prosperity of the community which is stressed, not prosperity of the individual.

For that reason, the economy is organised as a common efforts, based upon ways of working that accord with the family principle. The co-operative is the form of enterprise in harmony with this.

The economy is based upon economic democracy, prosperity is for everybody. Therefore, branches of production which are important for the state and which affect the life of most people should be under the control of the State. If they are not, the top management of production will fall into the hands of individuals who are in power and numbers of the people will be oppressed by them.

Only those enterprises which do not affect the life of most people may be in the hands of individuals.

The earth and waters and the natural riches contained therein are the fundamentals of the people's prosperity. Therefore, they should be controlled by the State and be made use of for the greatest possible prosperity for the people.

*Article 34.*

Already clear enough; see above.

**Chapter XV. Flag and Language**

*Article 35.*

Already clear.

*Article 36.*

Already clear.

In the areas possessing languages of their own which are actively used by the people concerned (for instance, Javanese, Sundanese, Madurese, and so forth), those languages will be respected and also cared for by the State.

Those languages are a part of the living culture of Indonesia.

**Chapter XVI. Alternations to the Constitution**

*Article 37.*

Already clear.

Whereas, with the support of the majority of the people of Indonesia, and impelled by our own conviction, we are forced to follow the one and only way of saving the State of the Proclamation,

Whereas we are convinced that the Djakrta Charter dated 22nd June 1945 gave inspiration to the 1945 Constitution and constitutes one link in a single chain with that Constitution;

Therefore, on the grounds mentioned above.

We, President of the Republic of Indonesia, Supreme Commander of the Armed Forces, Decree the dissolution of the Constituent Assembly. Decree that the 1945 Constitution be in force again for the whole of the Indonesian People and the entire native land of Indonesia as from the date of this Decree, and that the Provisional Constitution be no longer in force.

The setting up of the Provisional Majelis Permusyawaratan Rakyat which shall be composed of the members of the dewan Perwakilan Rakyat augmented by delegates from the regional territories and from the groups, as well as the setting up of the Provisional Supreme Advisory Council, will be executed in the shortest possible time.

Decreed at Djakrta on 5th July 1959

In the Name of the People of Indonesia

President of the Republic of Indonesia, Supreme Commander of the Armed Forces.

SUKARNO.

# Bibliography

## Books


Abdulgani, Roeslan, Pancasila: The Prime Mover of the Indonesian Revolution, Jakarta: Prapanca, 1958.

Anderson, Benedict, Mythology and the Tolerance of the Javanese, Ithaca: Modern Indonesian Project, Cornell University, 1965.

________, Java in a Time of Revolution, Ithaca: Cornell University Press, 1972.

Anderson, Benedict and Ruth McVey, A Preliminary Analysis of the October 1, 1965 Coup in Indonesia, Ithaca: Cornell University, Modern Indonesia Project, 1971.

Apter, David, "Introduction." In Ideology and Discontent, ed. David Apter, New York: Free Press of Glencoe, 1964.

Barton, Greg, "The Impact of Neo-Modernism on Indonesian Islamic Thought: The Emergence of a New Pluralism," In Bourchier and Legge, eds. Democracy in Indonesia: 1950s and 1990s, Clayton, Victoria: Centre of Southeast Asian Studies, Monash University, 1994.

Benda, Harry J. The Crescent and the Rising Sun: Indonesian Islam under Japanese Occupation. The Hague: W. Van Hoeve Ltd., 1958.

_______, "Prefatory Note." In Ideology in Indonesia: Sukarno's Indonesian Revolution, Donald E. Weathaerbee. Yale University: Southeast Asia Monograph Series No.8, 1966.

Boland, B.J. The Struggle of Islam in Modern Indonesia, The Hague: Martinus Nijhoff, 1971, Slightly revised reprint, 1982.

Bouchier, David and John Legge, eds. Democracy in Indonesia: 1950s and 1990s, Clayton, Victoria: Centre of Southeast Asian Studies, Monash University, 1994.

Budiman, Arief, ed. State and Civil Society in Indonesia, Clayton, Victoria: Centre for Southeast Asian Studies, Monash University, 1990.

Cribb, Robert, ed. The Indonesian Killings 1965-1966: Studies From Java and Bali, Clayton, Victoria: Centre for Southeast Asian Studies, Monash University, 1990.

______, The Army and Politics in Indonesia, Ithaca: Cornell University Press, 1978.

Crouch, Harold and Hal Hill, eds. Indonesian Assessment 1992: Political Perspectives on the 1990s, Canberra: Australian National University, 1992.

Dahm, Bernhard, Sukarno and the Struggle for Indonesian Independence, Ithaca: Cornell University Press, 1969.

______, History of Indonesia in the Twentieth Century, London: Pall Mall Press, 1971.

Darmaputera, Eka, Pancasila and the Search for Identity and Modernity in Indonesian Society: A Cultural and Ethical Analysis, Leiden: E.J. Brill, 1988.

Douglas, Stephen A, Political Socialization and Student Activism in Indonesia, Urbana: University of Illinois Press, 1970.

Driyakara, S.I., East Timor: The November 12 Massacre and its Aftermath, New York: Asia Watch, December 1991.

Emmerson, Donald K., Indonesia's Elite: Political culture and Cultural Politics, Ithaca: Cornell University Press, 1976.

Fealy, Greg and Greg Barton, eds. Nahdlatul Ulama: Traditional Islam and Modernity, Clayton, Victoria: Centre of Southeast Asian Studies, Monash University, 1995.

Federspiel, Howard M., Muslim Intellectuals and National Development in Indonesia, New York: Nova Science Publishers, 1992.

Feith, Herbert, The Decline of Constitutional Democracy in Indonesia, Ithaca: Cornell University Press, 1962.

Feith, Herbert and Lance Castles, eds, Indonesian Political Thinking 1945-1965, Ithaca: Cornell University Press, 1970.

Geertz, Clifford. "The Javanese Village." In Local, Ethnic, and National Loyalties in Village Indonesia, ed. G Skinner, Ithaca: Cornell University Modern Indonesia Project, 1959.

______, The Religion of Java, Glencoe, Illinois: The Free Press, 1960.

______, "Ideology as a Cultural system." In Ideology and Discontent, ed. David Apter, New York: Free Press of Glencoe, 1964.

Gluck, Carol, Japan's Modern Myths: Ideology in the late Meiji Period, Princeton: Princeton University, 1985.

Hatta, Mohammed, Memoir, Jakarta, Tintamas, 1978.

Hindley, Donald, The Communist Party of Indonesia, 1951-1963. Berkeley: University of California Press, 1966.

Holt, Claire, ed. Culture and Politics in Indonesia, London: Cornell University Press, 1972.

Hooker, M.B., ed. Islam in Southeast Asia, Leiden: E.J., Brill, 1983.

Human Rights in Indonesia and East Timor: The Limits of Openness, New York: Human Rights Watch/Asia, September 1994.

Jackson, Karl D. and Lucian W. Pye, eds. Political Power and communication in Indonesia, Berkeley: University of California Press, 1978.

Jenkins, David, Suharto and his Generals: Indonesian Military Politics, 1975-1983, Ithaca: Cornell University Modern Indonesia Project, 1984.

Jha, Ganganath, Ethnic Politics in Southeast Asia and Quest for Identity, New Delhi, NBO, 1998.

Kahin, George McT, Nationalism and Revolution in Indonesia, Ithaca: Cornell University Press, 1952.

Lane, Max, "Openness," Political Discontent and Succession in Indonesia: Political Developments in Indonesia, 1989-91, Nathan, Queensland: Centre for the Study of Australia-Asia Relations, Griffith University, 1991.

Lee, Khoon Choy, A Fragile Nation: The Indonesian Crisis, Singapore World Scientific, 1999.

Legge, J.D, Sukarno, A Political Biography, Harmondsworth, Middlesex: Penguin Books, 1972.

Lev, Daniel, The Transition to Guided Democracy, Indonesian Politics, 1957-1959, Ithaca: Cornell University Modern Indonesia Project, 1966.

Liddle, R. William, Politics and Culture in Indonesia, Ann Arbor: Center for Political Studies, Institute for social Research, University of Michigan, 1988.

______, "Improvising Political Cultural Change: Three Indonesian Cases." In James Schiller ed., Indonesian Political Culture: Asking the Right Questions, Athens, Ohio: Ohio University Center for Southeast Asian Studies, forthcoming.

McDonald, Hamish, Suharto's Indonesia, Blackburn, Victoria: Fontana, 1980.

Macie, J.A.C. "The Golkar Victory and party-Aliran Alignments." In Indonesia After the 1971 Elections, ed. Ocy Hong Lee, London: Oxford University Press, 1974.

Macie, Jamie, "Economic Growth and Depoliticization." In Driven by Growth: Political Change in the Asia-Pacific Region, ed. James W. Morely, Armonk, New York: M.E. Sharpe, 1993.

Moertopo, Ali, The Acceleration and Modernization of 25 Years' Development, Jakarta; Yavasan Proklamasi, Center for Strategic and International Studies, 1972.

Morfit, Michael, "Pancasila Orthodoxy." In Central Government and Local Development in Indonesia, ed. Colın MacAndrews, Singapore: Oxford University Press, 1986.

Mortimer, Rex, Indonesian Communism Under Sukarno: Ideology and Politics, 1959-1965, Ithaca: Cornell University Press, 1974.

Nasution, Adnan Buyung, The Aspiration for Constitutional Government in Indonesia: A Socio-Legal Study of the Indonesian Konstituante, 1956-1959, Jakarta: Sinar Harapan, 1992.

Nasution, Abdul Haris, Pancasila Democracy Today and Tomorrow, Jakarta: Provisional People's Consultative Assembly, 1972.

Noer, Deliar, The Modernist Muslim Movement in Indonesia, 1900-1942, Singapore; Oxford University Press, 1973.

Notosuanto, Nugroho and Ismael Saleh, The coup Attempt of the "September 30th Movement" in Indonesia, Jakarta: Pembimbing Masa, 1968.

Pabottingi, Mochtar, "Indonesia: Historicizing the New Order's Legitimacy Dilemma." In Muthiah Alagappa, ed. Political Legitimacyin southeast Asia: Quest for Moral Authority, stanford: Stanford University Press, 1995.

Pauker, Guy, "The Role of the military in Indonesia." In The Role of the Military in Underdeveloped Countries, ed. J.J. Johnson, Princeton: Princeton University Press, 1962.

Penders, C.L.M. and Ulf sundhaussen, Abdul Haris Nasution, A Political biography,St. Lucia, Queensland: University of Queensland Press, 1985.

Ramage, Douglas E., Politics in Indonesia, London, Routledge, 1995.

Reeve, David, Golkar of Indonesia: An Alternative to the Party System, Singapore: Oxford University Press, 1985.

Ricklefs, M.C., A History of Indonesia, Bloomington: Indiana University Press, 1981.

Robinson, Richard, Indonesia: The Rise of Capital, Sydney: Allen & Unwin, 1986.

Said, Salim, the Genesis of Power: General Sudirman and the Indonesian Military in Politics, 1945-1949. Singapore: Institute of southeast Asian Studies, 1992.

Schiller, James, ed., Indonesian political Culture: Asking the Right Questions, Athens, Ohio University, Center for Southeast Asian Studies, forthcoming.

Schwarz, Adam, A Nation in Waiting: Indonesia in the 1990s, Sydney: Allen & Unwin, and Boulder: Westview Press, 1994.

Scott, James C., Political Ideology in Malaysia: Reality and the Beliefs of an Elite, New Haven: Yale University Press, 1968.

Sjadzali, Munawir, Islam and Governmental System: Teachings, History and Reflection, Jakarta: Indonesia-Netherlands Cooperation in Islamic Studies, 1991.

______, Muslims' Interests are Better Served in the Absence of Muslim parties (The Indonesian Experience). Jakarta: Ministry of Religious Affairs, 1992.

Students Jailed for Puns, Asia Watch Report (March 1993).

Sukarno, Pancasila: The Basis of the State of the Republic of Indonesia, Jakarta: National Committee for the Commemoration of the Birth of Pancasila, 1964.

Sundhaussen, Ulf, The Road to Power: Indonesian Military Politcs 1945-1967, Kuala Lumpur: oxford University Press, 1982.

______, "Indonesia: Past and Present Encounters with Democracy." In Democracy in Developing Countries, Volume Three: Aisa, eds. Larry Diamond, Juan J. Linz, and Seymour Martin Lipset, 423-474. Boulder: Lynne Rienner, 1989.

Van Dijk, C., Rebellion Under the Banner of Islam: The Darul Islam in Indonesia, the Hague: Martinus Nihjoff, 1981.

Vatikkiotis, Michael, Indonesian Politics Under Suharto: Order, Development and Pressure for Change, London: Routledge, 1993.

Von der Mehden, Fred, Religion and Modernization in Southeast Asia, Syracuse; Syracuse University Press, 1986.

Warren, Carol, "Balinese Political Culture and Rhetoric of National Development." In Creating Indonesian Cultures, ed. Paul Alexander, 39-54, Sydney: Oceania Publications, 1989.

Weatherbee, Donald E., Ideology in Indonesia, Sukarno's Indonesian Revolution, Yale University: Southeast Asia Monograph Series No.8. 1966.

______, "The Consolidation of the Pancasila State," The Asia Society, New York, November 11, 1985.

Zoetmulder, P.J., The Cultural Background of Indonesian politics, Columbia: Institute of International Studies, University of South Carolina, 1967.

## Articles

Arndt, H.W., "Transmigration: Achievements, problems", Bulletin of Indonesian Economic Studies, Vol. 19, No.3, 1983, pp. 50-73.

Arndt, H.W. and Sundaram, R.M., "Transmigration: Land Settlement or Regional Development" Bulletin of Indonesia Economic Studies, Vol. 13, No.3, 1977, pp. 72-90.

Awanohara, Susumu, "Stand-off in Jakarta", Far Eastern Economic Review, 26 April, 1984, pp. 18-19.

Awanohara, Susuma and Reinhardt, "Under two flags", Far Eastern Economic Review, 15 March 1984, p. 46.

Baker, Mark, "A triumph that turned sour", Far Eastern Economic Review, 3 November 1978, pp. 26-27.

Banerjee, D, "Insurgencies in Southeast Asia: implications for India," Strategic Analysis, Vol. 14, No. 1, April 1990, pp. 45-48.

Bell, Ian Feith, Herb and Hatley, Ron, "The West Papuan Challenge to Indonesian Authority in Irian: Old Problems, New Possibilities", Asian survey, Vol. 26, No. 5, May 1986, pp. 539-554.

Birth, Anthony H, "Minority Nationalist Movements and Theories of Integration", World Politics, Vol. 20, No. 3, 1978, pp. 325-44.

Bohane, Ben, "Continuing the Struggle: A New Rebel Leadership Rises in Irian Jaya", Asia Week 30 July 1999, p. 22.

Bowen, John R., "On the Political construction of Tradition: Gotong-Royong in Indonesia", Journal of Asian Studies 45 (1986), pp. 545-561.

Brown, David, "From Peripheral communities to Ethnic Nations: Separatism in South East Asia", Pacific Affairs, vol. 61, No. 1, Spring 1988, pp. 51-57.

Callick, Rowan, "Rebels without a home", Far Eastern Economic Review, October 1982, p. 12.

Deutsch, Karl, W., "Social mobilisation and Political Development, American Political Science Review, Vol. 55, September 1976, pp. 493-514.

Emmerson, Donald K., "Understanding the New Order: Bureaucratic pluralism in Indonesia", Asian Survey 23, No. 11, November 1983, pp. 1220-1241.

Gareth N. Jones, "Soekarno's Early views upon territorial boundaries", Australian Outlook, Vol. 18, No. 1, April 1984, pp. 22-34.

Goode C., "Papua and New Guinea's West Irian: A Review of 1969", Australian Territory, vol. 10, No. 11, 1970, pp. 25-31.

Gordon, B.K., "The Potential for Indonesia's Expansionism", Pacific Affair's Vol. 36, 1963-64, pp. 378-394.

Gunn, Geoffrey L, "Ideology and the Concept of government in the Indonesian New Order", Asian Survey XIV, No. 8, August 1979, pp. 751-769.

Hader, Leon T., "What Green Peril", Foreign Affairs, Vol. 72, No. 2 (Spring 1993), pp. 27-42.

Hardjono, John, "Assisted and Unassisted Transmigration in the context of Repelita III Targets", Prisma 18, September 1980, pp. 3-16.

Harper, Noorman, "West New Guinea: An Australian View", International Studies, New Delhi, Vol. III, No. 1, October 1961, pp. 109-131.

Hary, Premesta and Herbert Feith and Daniel. Lev., "The End of Indonesian Rebellion" Pacific Affairs, Vol. 36, Spring 1963, pp. 32-46.

Hastings, Peter, "Papua New Guinea – Defence under Attack", Far Eastern Economic Review, 23 June 1983, p. 44.

Jan Van somseren, "Indonesia's upside – down and reform", Tapol Bulletin No. 67, January 1985, pp. 16-18.

Kim, Hyung – Jun, "Changing interpretation of religious freedom in Indonesia", Journal of South East Asian Studies, September 1998, pp. 357-73.

Kilvert, Andrew, "West Papua mobilising for freedom from Indonesia", Pacific Islands, February 2000, pp. 36-37.

Leigh, Barbara, "Making the Indonesian State: the Role of School Texts", Review of Indonesian and Malaysian Affairs 25, No. 1 Winter 1991.

Liddle, R. William, "Indonesia's Democratic Past and Future", Comparative Politics, July 1992, pp. 443-462.

______, "Indonesia's Threefold Crisis", Journal of Democracy 3, No. 4, October 1992.

Liefer, Michael, "challenge of creating a civil society in Indonesia", Indonesian Quarterly, December 1995, pp. 354-60.

Luwarso, Lukas, "Liberation of the Indonesian Press" Development dialogue, 1948, pp. 85-95.

McFetridge, Charles Donald, "SESKOAD – Training the Elite", Indonesia, No. 36, October 1983, pp. 87-98.

Macqueen, Norman, "Papua New Guinea's relations with Indonesia and Australia: Diplomacy on the Asia – Pacific Interface", Asian Survey, 20, No. 5, May 1989, pp. 530-41.

May, R.J., "Religious factor in three minority movements: The Moro of the Phillippines, the Malay's of Thailand and Indonesia's West Papuans", Contemporary South East Asia, No. 13(4), March 1992, pp. 396-414.

May, R.J., "Mutual Respect, Friendship and co-operation?", "The Indonesia Papua New Guinea Border and its effects on Relations between

Papua New Guinea and Indonesia", Bulletin of concerned Asian Scholars, Vol. 19, No. 4, October-December 1987, pp. 7-12.

Miller, Judith, "The Challenge of Radical Islam", Foreign Affairs, Vol. 12, No. 2 Spring 1993, pp. 43-56. Moeljarto, Vidhyandika and Gad and VH, Arya budhisastra, "Indonesia in transition: Government response to the reform demands in the state of uncertainty, "Indonesian Quarterly, 26,3, 1998, pp. 1183-1205.

Moertopo, Ali, "Some Basic Considerations in 25 Years Development", Indonesian Quarterly 1, No. 1, October 1972.

Morfit, Michael, "Pancasila: The Indonesian State Ideology", Asian Survey XXI, No. 8, August 1981.

Pauker, Guy J., "Indonesia at fifty", Orbis, 40, No. 3, Summer 1996, pp. 445-57.

Premdas, R.R., "Papua New Guinea in 1985", Asian Survey, Vol. XXVI, No. 2, February, 1986, pp. 196-206.

Ramos-horta, Jose, "Self determination for East Timor: Implications for the Region", Australian Journal of International Affairs, 57, No. 1, April 1997, pp. 97-102.

Rohdewohld, Rainer, "Government reforms in developing countries: The case of Indonesia", Indian Journal of Public Administration, 43, No. 2, April-June 1997, pp. 181-208.

Salame, Ghassan, "Islam and the West", Foreign policy, No. 90, Spring 1993, 22-37.

Seth, S.P., "Indonesia: A Regional Tinder Box", Economic and Political Weekly, Vol. 34, No. 19, 8-14, May 1999, pp. 1078-79.

Schwarz, Adam, "Indonesia after Suharto", Foreign Affairs, 76 No. 4, July-August 1997, pp. 119-34.

Schwaarz, Adam, "Irian Jaya seeks bigger say in its own destiny: Eastern Approach" Far Eastern Economic Review, 11 July 1991, pp. 23-25.

Soeasastro, Hadi, "The Political Economy of Deregulation in Indonesia", Asian Survey 29, No. 9, September 1989, pp. 853-869.

Soewartoyo, "Internal migration between Java – Bali and Eastern Indonesia" Indonesian Quaterly, 24 No.3 1996; pp. 303-22.

Tengku Hassan M. di Teero, "Indonesia Bastion of Colonialism" Freedom at Issuel, July-August, 1983, pp. 18-20.

Thopson, Herb and Duggie James, "Political economy of the forestry industry in Indonesia", Journal of Contemporary Asia, 26 No.3, 1996, pp. 352-65.

Tyiptoherijanto, Prijono, "Poverty and Inequality in Indonesia at the end of the 20th Century", Indonesia quarterly 25 No. 3 1997, pp. 251-75.

Van der Kroef, J.M, "West New Guinea: The Uncertain Future" Asian Survey, Vol.8, 1968, pp. 691-707.

Van den Han Allert, "Development Co-operation and Human Rights: Indonesia – Dutch Controversy", Asian Survey, 33 No. 55 May 1993, pp. 531-39.

Vittorio, Lankunari, "Ethnocentrism and Ideology", Ethnic and Racial Studies, Vol.3, No.1, January 1980, pp.26-28.

Wahid, Abdurrahman, "The Islamic Masses in the Life of State and Nation", Prisma, No. 35 (March 1985): 3-10.

Walker, Connor, "Eco or Ethno Nationalism", Ethnic and Racial Studies, Vol.7, No.3, July 1984, pp. 324-54.

Williams, Malcolm Gault, "Organisasi Papua Merdeka, The Free Papua Movement Lives", Bulletin of Concerned Asian Scholars, Vol.19, No.4 October-December 1987, pp. 32-43.

# Index

Deep